Reading for Boys and Girls Illinois

A Subject Index and Annotated Bibliography

DOROTHY HINMAN
and RUTH ZIMMERMAN
for the
ILLINOIS STATE LIBRARY

AMERICAN LIBRARY ASSOCIATION
Chicago, 1970

ISBN 0-8389-0075-5 (1970)

Library of Congress Catalog Card Number 75-118853

Printed in the United States of America

Contents

Preface

The primary purpose of *Reading for Boys and Girls: Illinois* is to provide a reference tool which will help librarians, teachers, and boys and girls in Illinois quickly and efficiently locate library materials for a thorough and enjoyable study of their state. But it has a far wider use; young readers everywhere can learn much about America in general from the books that are listed in the Annotated Bibliography.

In these books are found the men, the motives, and the conditions responsible for the shaping of a great state and its destiny. The listed books were selected for the purpose of contributing an appreciation of our heritage and the growing need to conserve it. However, the information these books contain would be difficult to locate without a key. The Subject Index provides this. The appendixes furnish additional helps and consist of a list of suggested reference books, another of free and inexpensive materials, and a bibliography dealing with athletes and sports. There are no references to the appendixes in the Index except for two entries, "Athletes" and "Sports," which direct the reader to the bibliography on athletes and sports.

The list as a whole is somewhat unbalanced in grade-levels, subjects, and types of books. The scarcity of books for the lower four grades is unavoidable since so few are available. These are the grades, of course, in which the study of Illinois is least frequent. As to types of books, biography and fiction predominate. Among the many biographies, except for those of Abraham Lincoln, there are too few of outstanding nineteenth- and twentieth-century Illinoisans. Fiction is well represented. This is fortunate, for fiction often gives a better idea than informational books of the details of daily life and customs in a particular time and place.

Had books on all phases of the subject been plentiful, the list would have been more selective. Since this was not the case, and since there is a need for material on as many facets of life as possible, a few marginal books were included.

The compilers express their sincere appreciation to the many publishers who have generously aided them in this undertaking, and deep gratitude to their colleagues and friends who have given encouragement and patient help in countless ways.

Especial thanks are due Jennie White, friend, typist, and critic, for her endless hours of work and her enthusiastic, scholarly support.

DOROTHY HINMAN
RUTH ZIMMERMAN

Normal, Illinois
February, 1970

Introduction

From Illinois have come many personalities whose activities and contributions have made an impact reaching far beyond its borders, influencing movements of national and international scope. To study the history of the state is to view a kaleidoscopic pageantry of these men and movements. The early explorers of Illinois, its Indians, traders, religious and political leaders, soldiers, inventors, farmers, industrialists, workers, legislators, crusaders, philanthropists, idealists, authors, and artists crowd the scene and move in the shifting patterns of the development and expansion of religious, personal, and economic freedom, and of industry, trade, transportation, legislation, and culture.

Among those of national and international importance, two individuals of Illinois tower above all others—Abraham Lincoln and Adlai E. Stevenson. Illinois is called "the land of Lincoln," but Lincoln was greater than Illinois—he led his country in the effort to preserve the Union and forge a nation where there would be neither slave nor master. Stevenson was a citizen of Illinois, but he was also a "citizen of the world," as he called himself, and proved this by striving in the United Nations to carry out his ideal of a world at peace.

Not only its people but its geographical features tie Illinois to the nation and to the world. Her waterways beckoned to explorers, provided trade routes for Indians and traders, and contributed to the state's rapid industrial and economic growth. The two great waterways of Illinois are the Mississippi River, which forms the entire west boundary of the state, and Lake Michigan. The early explorers, Marquette, Joliet, and La Salle, realized the tremendous potential as a trade and transportation route of a river that flows past the mouth of the Missouri, gateway to the west, drains the great valley of the Ohio to the east, and empties into the Gulf of Mexico to the south. They also recognized that the area where many of the Mississippi's tributaries have their source, being near Lake Michigan, was a key location that could link the Gulf of the St. Lawrence River and thus to the Atlantic Ocean. Jean Baptiste Du Sable too recognized the unique qualities of the location, and founded a trading post on the shore of that lake. From that small beginning, Chicago has become the trading and transportation center of the nation.

The Mississippi flows through a fertile land which the John Deere plow and the McCormick reaper developed into an agricultural empire. This land is also rich in minerals—lead, zinc, oil, coal. Coal was the mineral which made possible the manufacturing necessitated by the growing demand for farm machinery. Now Illinois supplies many parts of this and other nations with minerals, farm machinery, and grain.

As the growth of Chicago justified the faith of its founder, men like Swift and Armour were lured to the city, making it a giant in the meat-packing industry. With the development of industries, trade and transportation became problems, for the freight shipments of grain, meat products, and machinery were too great a load for the natural waterways. Canals and railways were built to help carry that load. And so Chicago became the center for manufacture, trade, and transportation. Carl Sandburg, an Illinois poet, aptly called the city

> "Hog Butcher for the World,
> Tool Maker, Stacker of Wheat,
> Player with Railroads
>   and the Nation's Freight Handler."

To the factories and the farms and the mines came people from foreign lands, looking for freedom from want and tyranny.

Many found a new kind of oppression, for business, during that period of expansion, was exploiting both human and natural resources. The wretched working and living conditions of the workers produced crusaders for freedom who believed in "equality and justice for all"—crusaders like Jane Addams, Eugene Debs, and Clarence Darrow, who formed a vanguard in both state and national legislative battles for human rights and civil liberties. Burgeoning industry, accompanied by the influx of people and machines, has given the state new problems of congestion and housing, of management and labor, minority peoples and disadvantaged neighborhoods, land despoliation, and water and air pollution. All are problems typical of the other states of our country.

How to Use
the Subject Index
to Illinois Material

Introduction

In this Index specific page references are given to the subjects that are treated in the books listed in the Annotated Bibliography; these subjects are arranged in alphabetical order. In choosing subject entries for the Index, the compilers tried to select persons, places, and events important in the study of Illinois. To keep the Index within bounds, some specific subjects were omitted. For example, the entry "places to visit" is used rather than the specific "Field Museum" or "Brookfield Zoo."

For biographies and books of fiction a reference to the "whole book" indicates that the entire book deals with a particular person, area, period, or theme. In addition, there are page references given if, within the book, there is especially significant or interesting material about events or places or people. In the all too few informational books dealing with Illinois, most of which have their own indexes, just those indexes are usually given. In some instances, however, especially where there were numerous references for a given entry, the more important page numbers are listed after the word "index."

Since the span of Illinois history covers roughly three centuries, it seemed wise to divide the centuries into thirds—e.g., early 1800s, mid-1800s, late 1800s. Except for fiction, "mid-1900s" was not used to indicate the present period. Where a long time-span is treated, as, for example, under the "Chicago" and "Illinois" entries, the most recent period is listed first and the earlier periods follow in chronological order. In other instances, historical periods appear chronologically as subheads under the main entry.

How to use the Subject Index
to Illinois Material

Locating material on Black Hawk will serve as an example of how to use this Index. Begin by consulting the entry "Black Hawk" on page 8 in the Index, where the references begin as follows:

> Black Hawk, 18:whole book (index); 33:index, 27; 37:whole book, *10*; 40:148–63

The numbers which stand before the colons—18, 33, 37, 40—are the book numbers given in the Author-Title Key beginning on page 40 and in the Annotated Bibliography, which begins on page 48. To learn only the author and title of a book, refer to the corresponding number in the Key. For more detailed information about a book, refer to the corresponding number in the Annotated Bibliography.

The information which follows a colon indicates whether the book has an index, whether the whole book treats the given topic, and whether there are illustrations. The pages on which illustrations appear are in *italic* type. If the book has no index, specific page references are given. The semicolon marks the end of the references to each book.

Thus, for the references on Black Hawk listed above:

> 18 is the book number, which in the Author-Title Key is *Black Hawk* by Beckhard. The whole book is about Black Hawk, and the book has an index, as indicated by the word "index" in parentheses.

33 is the book number for *Illinois: From Its Glorious Past to the Present* by Carpenter. This book has its own index, which will locate the pages giving information about Black Hawk. The italic number indicates that page *27* has an illustration depicting Black Hawk.

37 is Cleven's *Black Hawk: Young Sauk Warrior*. The whole book is about Black Hawk, and there is an illustration of Black Hawk on page 10.

40 is *Fighting Indians of America* by Cooke. Since it has no index, the numbers 148–63 indicate the pages where material on Black Hawk will be found.

Other items that may be included in an entry are the following:

The symbol "SR" which means "scattered references," an indication that a book has no index and contains occasional bits of worthwhile information which are not sufficient to justify a page-listing for each.

The symbol (fic) which identifies books for fiction.

Except for the entries "Athletes" and "Sports," which refer to the sports bibliography on page 123, the Subject Index includes references only to the books listed in the Author-Title Key and in the more extensively treated Annotated Bibliography.

Subject Index
to Illinois Material

dex; **198**:18, 56–58, 97, 119–
21, 134–48 (fic)
campaign against Osage, **18**:
69–78
campaigns, **37**:149–87
early life, **37**:11–148
name, **37**:11–12, 108–10
Black Hawk Statue, **37**:*191*–92
Black Hawk War, **10**:78–79; **14**:
104–6; **18**:index; **26**:49–51;
34:index; **35**:37–41; **37**:
175–87; **40**:154–60; **43**:in-
dex; **61**:49; **87**:37–41; **93**:
88–89; **123**:34–36; **134**:130–
33; **147**:index; **198**:19–147
(fic)
Black Partridge, **99**:vi, 13–23
Blacks, **2**:whole book (fic); **34**:
index: **51**:whole book (fic);
82:108–17; **130**:whole book
(fic); *see also* Abolitionists;
Dunham, Katherine; Du Sa-
ble, Jean Baptiste; Lovejoy,
Owen; Slavery; Under-
ground Railroad
Blacksmith shop **171**:*42*, *46*–49
Bloomington, **33**:index; **178**:in-
dex
"Lost Speech," **154**:index
(mid-1800s), **93**:135; **100**:in-
dex; **123**:71
(early 1900s), **190**:32–75, 117–
30, 140–43
Boats, **8**:123–30, 138–41; **42**:14–
34
barges, **6**:index
canal boats, **8**:128–35
flatboats, **6**:index; **14**:82–87,
84; **48**:16–17, 37–42; **117**:
index, *17, 19*; **133**:*26*
keelboats, **6**:index; **23**:93–94;
54:52–56; **117**:index, *42*
lake freighters, **98**:142–45, *144*;
106:38–46
packets, **6**:index; **42**:17–29
rafts, **6**:index

shanty boats, **6**:index
showboats, **6**:index; **109**:*41*;
118:index, *66–67*
side-wheelers, **6**:index; **109**:
38; **133**:*39*
snag boats, **6**:index; **42**:36;
109:index; *see also* Snags
steamboats, **6**:whole book; **8**:
128–35; **109**:index; **118**:
index, *24–26, 29, 42*
construction of, **118**:index
crew, **118**:index
glossary of, **118**:94
races, **6**:index; **118**:79–88
stern-wheelers, **6**:index; **109**:*39*
store boats, **117**:index, *45*
towboats, **6**:index; **42**:29–34;
109:index
Bogue, Captain Vincent, **154**:
index
Bogus Island, **24**:148–49; **155**:
32–33
Bond, Shadrach, **31**:index
Books and reading (late 1800s),
94:20; **174**:28, 41–51; **167**:
51–52, 74
Bounty (on animals), **4**:3–4
Bowen, Louise de Koven, **69**:67,
105, 116–17; **94**:83–93, 123;
197:233–38
Bowen Country Club, **69**:116–17;
94:123; **136**:144–46, *145*;
197:123–25, *186*
Bowen Hall, **69**:105; **94**:104
Bowman, Joseph, **73**:41–70, 94–
120; **149**:index
Bridges, **6**:index; *see also* Eads
Bridge
Brown, George W., **52**:5–6
Buffalo Rock, **3**:85; **70**:71; *see
also* Kaskaskia Indians—vil-
lage on the Illinois (La Van-
tum)
Burial mounds, **156**:index
Burnham, Daniel, **60**:index; **84**:

9

10

12

14

Herndon, Rowan, **49**:54–56, 64–68, 75–76; **93**:87, 90

Herndon, William (Billy), **10**: 105–6, 156; **26**:64–66; **43**: index; **49**:217–19; **61**:63–65, 76; **93**:119, 124, 145, 160; **100**:index; **123**:56–58, 62, 71, 88; **129**:92, 96, 101; **133**:index, *41*; **147**:index; **154**:index; **163**:index

Hickok, James (Wild Bill), **4**: whole book; **67**:index; **85**: whole book
  early life, **85**:3–20
  in Illinois, **4**:1–15, 164–75

"Hickory Buds," **100**:164

Hill, Samuel, **49**:34, 46, 75, 77–79, 99–104, 129–30, 141, 144

Hillman, Sidney,
  in Illinois, **176**:142–47, *143*, 240–41

Historic trails, **34**: map *140*

History, **11**:9–11; **16**:11–20; **33**: whole book (index); **34**: whole book (index); **102**: whole book (index); *see also* Illinois; also under specific subject, as Chicago fire (1871); Dearborn Massacre; Voyageurs

Hodenasates (Sauk dwellings), **198**:88

Holidays, **16**:list 39; **175**:91–101

Home life (mid-1800s), **4**:6–10

Homes
  (mid-1800s), **88**:17–26; **171**: *36, 38, 42*
  (late 1800s), **99**:127–28; **174**: 20–32

Homes and furnishings (early 1800s), **49**:86

Hopewellian culture, **156**:index
  artifacts, **156**:insert after *53*

Hopewellians, **8**:10–12; **34**:31; **138**:index

Horses, Indians' use of, **18**:42–47, 88–92; **156**:86–88

Houseboat life, **115**:1–29

Housing (late 1800s), **94**:110–12; **197**:156–63

Hubbard, Gurdon, **12**:SR (fic); **49**:152; **99**:33–39, 110–11; **103**:index

Hull House, **69**:57–71; **74**:index, *57*; **94**:54–68, *59*, 75–80, 122; **96**:92–97; **124**:62–68; **136**:index, *61, 66, 74*; **142**: index; **159**:33–69; **165**:index; **189**:180–91, *181*; **197**: 127–32, *130, 198, 210, 222*, 240
  fortieth anniversary, **197**:222–25
  services of, **94**:68–74, 80–83, 95–105; **189**:184–90; **197**: 130–202, 216–44

Hunting, *see* Industries—hunting

Hustin, Katherine, **30**:whole book (fic)

Icarians, **33**:index

Illinois, **11**:whole book; **16**:whole book; **33**:whole book (index); **34**:whole book (index); **77**:index; **102**:whole book (index); *see also* Courts; Documents; Government; Governors; Rural life; State departments; State officers; State symbols
  counties, list of, **102**:186–88
  county of Virginia **149**:index
  French in, **11**:6–8; **34**:43–48, *45, 47*; *see also* French in Illinois
  history, chronology of, **33**:85; **34**:192–94
  name, origin of, **11**:5; **34**:34

Illinois (late 1600s), **28**:14–25
  (early 1800s), **61**:41–42; **63**: whole book (fic); **93**:67,

99; **134**:98–104
cost of living, **61**:45
countryside, 9:178–79
(mid-1800s), **10**:129–30; **88**:
whole book (fic); **89**:
whole book (fic); **90**:162–
76, 198; **126**:whole book
(fic); **128**:168–92; **147**:68
(late 1800s), **166**:whole book
(fic)
(mid-1900s), **194**:whole book
(fic)
Illinois Assembly (1830s), **154**:
index
Illinois Commission on Occupa-
tional Diseases, **74**:16, 75, 89
Illinois Confederacy, *see* Indians
—Illinois Confederacy
Illinois Institute for Juvenile Research, **132**:index
Illinois River, 3:83–89; **8**:whole
book (index), map before
p.1; **34**:index; **45**:155–60;
48:66–72; **49**:28–30; **64**:
101–261 (fic); **70**:99–100;
131:75, 84–86, 92–93; **141**:
146–48; **150**:index; **185**:35,
67–71, 106–9
conservation areas, **8**:164–67
pollution, **8**:159–63
problems (1900s), **8**:157–63
sports, **8**:170–78
transportation, **8**:121–35
wildlife, **8**:156–67, 170–71
Illinois River area (places to visit),
8:164–71, 178
Illinois State Natural History
Society, **196**:index
Illinois State Normal University,
196:index
Illinois Territory, **16**:3; **34**:52–53;
102:23
Illinois Thirty-first Regiment,
167:22–26, 54–55, 132–33
Illinois Wesleyan University,
196:index

Immigrants, **34**:index; **94**:55–56,
106–14; **102**:index; **136**:53–
57, 112–20; **197**:149–55,
174–77, 183–85, 191–97,
219–24, 238–40
in Chicago (late 1800s), **69**:
56–63, 73–74
Important people, *see* Famous
people; *see also* names of
individuals, e.g., Du Sable,
Jean Baptiste; Fermi, En-
rico; Lovejoy, Elijah
Indian Creek Massacre, **17**:199–
200; **49**:22–24
Indian League, **18**:index; *see also*
Unification, Indian
Indian legends, **48**:78–80
Indian mounds, *see* Mound Builders; Mounds
Indian tribes, *see under* individual
tribes, as Kaskaskia, Kicka-
poo, Ottawa, Peoria, Potawatomi, Sauk and Fox, Win-
nebago Indians
Indians, **8**:12–13, 22–97; **11**:in-
dex; **16**:12, 15–16; **23**:in-
dex; **33**:index; **34**:index; **38**:
211–17; **45**:44–56, 106–22,
155–60, 179–84; **75**:43; **101**:
11–14, 90–100; **102**:index;
103:index; **105**:131–37; **131**:
index; **165**:43–46
burial mounds, **156**:index
customs, **3**:87–88; **23**:13–15;
131:59–64
dances (calumet), **45**:116–18;
131:61–64, *63*
food, **3**:87–88; **45**:115–19; **101**:
97–99; **131**:58
Illinois confederacy, **156**:ix
peace pipes, *see* Calumets
sports, **38**:212
trade, **17**:48–62; **18**:50–56, 82–
86, 92–95
trails, **34**:145–46; **156**:index

23

56, 62–64, 79–80, 87, 91–92; **129**:86–90, 113–16; **133**:index, *48*, *112*, *132–33*; **147**: index; **151**:index; **154**:index, *118*; **163**:whole book (index), *90*; **164**:78–79

Lincoln, Robert, **10**:157; **26**:67, 84; **43**:index; **49**:214–15, 230; **61**:61, 76; **93**:119–52; **123**:56–83; **147**:index; **164**: 81–82, 89–90

Lincoln, Sarah Bush, **9**:whole book; **10**:127, 150–53; **14**: 135–41; **43**:index; **49**:35–37, 227–29, 247; **57**:SR 195–282; **61**:76; **93**:160; **123**: 87–88; **129**:52–54; **133**:index, *15*; **147**:index; **154**:index; **164**:56

in Illinois, **9**:173–223

home in Coles County, **65**:*94*

Lincoln, Thomas, **9**:182–213; **57**: SR 195–246; **61**:41–42

Lincoln, Thomas (Tad), **10**:125, 157; **26**:84; **43**:index; **49**: 230–31; **61**:77; **93**:129, 148, 152; **123**:80; **133**:index, *112*; **147**:index; **164**:83–86; **191**: whole book

Lincoln, William (Willie), **10**: 125, 157; **26**:84; **43**:index; **49**:230–31; **61**:77; **93**:129, 148, 152; **123**:80; **133**:index, *113*; **147**:index; **164**:81–90

Lincoln-Douglas debates *see* Lincoln, Abraham—debates with Douglas

Lindsay, Vachel, **20**:index; **180**: 199–209; *see also* Authors

in Illinois, **20**:104–12, insert after *64*

Linn, Ben, **149**:index

Literature, **16**:77–79

Little Egypt (nickname for Southern Illinois), **89**:whole

book (fic); **162**:whole book (fic); **166**:whole book (fic); **167**:whole book (fic)

Locks and dams, **109**:index

Loeb, Richard, **76**:index; **145**:index

Loeb-Leopold case, **76**:index; *see also* Darrow, Clarence —cases and trials

Logan, Colonel John, **167**:SR whole book (fic)

Logan, Stephen, **26**:61–64; **43**: index; **49**:185, 216–17; **93**: 90, 114, 145; **100**:index; **129**:76; **133**:index, *41*; **147**: index

"Logrolling," **154**:index

Long Knives, **135**:index, *56*; *see also* Big Knives; Clark, George Rogers

Long Nine, **34**:index; **43**:index; **49**:151–56; **93**:103–4; **123**: 50; **151**:index; **154**:105

Loop (Chicago), **34**:index; **103**: index; **165**:index

"Lost Speech," *see* Lincoln, Abraham—speeches

Loud Thunder, **18**:index

Louisiana Purchase, *see* National events, effect on Illinois

Lovejoy, Elijah, **34**:index; **43**:index; **49**:163–64; **125**:43–60, *44*; **129**:84; **132**:index; **147**: index

Lovejoy, Owen, **8**:index

Loyalty oaths, **178**:index

McCormick, Cyrus, **97**:whole book; **103**:index

early life, **97**:2–49

employees, provision for, **97**: 145, 154–55

honors won, **97**:96–98, 109–17, 122–23, 138–55

in Illinois, **97**:96–156, *152*

philanthropy, **97**:132–38, 145

28

Mississippi culture, 156:index
Mississippi River, 34:index; 45:
    68–74, 99–106, 121–26; 48:
    73–90; 102:index; 109:whole
    book (index)
  channel and channel control,
    109:index
  floods and flood control, 109:
    index
  legends, 6:126–33
  name, origin of, 6:38; 54:34;
    109:index
  trade, 6:31–32
  transportation, 109:index
Modoc Rock Shelter, 8:index
Monk's Mound (Cahokia), 33:in-
    dex; 34:index; 102:14–15;
    156:index
Monso (Iroquois), 3:92, 97–98;
    70:74; 150:index
Montgomery Ward and Com-
    pany, 13:53–103, 111–112
Montgomery Ward Catalogue,
    13:86–95
Mormon Church, 29:index; 104:
    index
Mormon Temple (Nauvoo), 29:
    58–59, 78, 82–90; 34:59;
    104:22, 62
Mormon Trail, 104:map 54
Mormons, 16:16; 30:11–64 (fic);
    33:index; 34:index; 92:whole
    book; 151:index
  in Illinois, 92:9–14, 26–31;
    104:3–38, 60–62
Morris, Nelson, 143:24, 31–36,
    151
Mother Bickerdyke, see Bicker-
    dyke, (Mother) Mary Ann
Mother Jones, see Jones, (Mother)
    Mary
Mound Builders, 16:12; 33:in-
    dex; 34:31; 102:14–15; 156:
    index
  artifacts, 138:78, 85, 86, 94,
    102, 109; 156:38, insert
    after 53
  mound sites, 138:78, 108, 113
Mounds, 8:171, 173; 34:30–33,
    32; 156:53; see also
    Cahokia; Dickson; Kincaid;
    Knight; Monk's; and Oak-
    wood Mounds
Mount Pulaski Courthouse, 65:
    76–77
Music, 16:73

Naromse, 18:index
National documents, effect on
    Illinois,
  Greenville Treaty (1795), 8:
    81; 34:51; 71:153–65;
    99:6
  Kansas-Nebraska Bill, 34:63–
    64; 43:70–71; 57:249–55;
    154:147–48
  Northwest Ordinance (1787),
    34:51; 71:148; 102:87
  St. Louis Treaty (1804), 16:
    15–16; 17:48–53; 18:in-
    dex; 37:162–64
National events, effect on Illinois,
  Abolitionist movement, 147:
    68–69
  Civil War, 34:68–71; 89:whole
    book (fic); 99:77–95; 102:
    28; 167:whole book (fic)
  French and Indian War, 71:
    48–49, 70
  Louisiana Purchase, 17:45–48
  Panic of 1837, 99:45
  Panic of 1893, 143:160–68;
    174:27–29
  Revolutionary War, 44:40–71;
    73:31–177; 135:23–28;
    149:68–146
  Spanish-American War, 174:
    162–69
National Grange, 13:77–86, 93–
    94

National Lead Company, **74**:index
Natural resources, **34**:index; **77**: 207–8; **102**:index
Nauvoo, **29**:index; **33**:index; **34**: index, 59–60; **104**:index; **151**:index
(mid-1800s), **30**:11–64 (fic)
Navy Pier (Chicago), **165**:index
Negroes, *see* Blacks
New Salem, **33**:index; **34**:index, map *171*; **65**:*22–71*; **87**: whole book; **133**:index, *32–33*
(early 1800s), **10**:65–66; **14**: 83–84, 89–90, 93–103; **36**:76; **43**:29–43; **48**:44–64; **49**:32–34, 37–49, 69–77, 128, 140–43; **57**:216–27; **61**:43–45; **93**:72–74; **121**:46–57; **123**:28–34, 38–50, 40–41; **129**:51–54; **134**:110–16, 120–25; **147**: index; **154**:index; **164**:56–58; **171**:*40–57*
residents of, **10**:65–66; **87**:13–14; **93**:78
(mid-1800s), **49**:160, 247
Newspapers, *see* Communication
Nicolay, John, **100**:index
North Pass, *see* Makanda
Northwest Ordinance (1787), *see* National documents, effect on Illinois
Northwest Territory, **16**:map *15*; **34**:index; **102**:index, map *22*

Oakwood Mound, **34**:index
Observer (Abolitionist newspaper), **132**:index; **147**:74
Offutt, Denton, **9**:182–83, 194–95; **10**:59–69, 77; **14**:80–88, 98–99, 104, 107; **26**:43–45, 50; **36**:75–79; **43**:index; **48**: 1–7, 17, 39–41, 44–50, 60–90; **49**:13–14, 32, 34,

40–46, 67; **57**:213–22; **93**: 70–82; **123**:28, 30; **129**:47–55, 59, 62; **133**:index; **134**: 105–13, 120–24; **147**:index; **154**:index
Ogden, William, **99**:44–55, 99; **103**:index; **120**:42–56
Ohio River, **25**:49–50; **115**:10–11, 16–21
O'Leary, Mrs. Catherine, **139**: index
Oliver, James, **97**:151
Olmstead, Frederick, **99**:138
Oquaka (mid-1800s), **27**:10–16
Ordinance of 1787, *see* National documents, effect on Illinois —Northwest Ordinance (1787)
Organizations (early 1800s), debating society, **49**:48–49 temperance society, **49**:48, 141
Osaukee (Osauki), *see* Kilbourne, Elijah
Ottawa Indians, **114**:202–4
Ouilmette, **71**:index; *see also* Wilmette
Owens, Mary, **10**:94; **49**:81–89, 142–49, 156–59, facing *91*, *155*; **93**:102–4, 110; **147**:index

Palmer, Potter, **99**:94–99, 122; **143**:56–58
Panic of 1837, *see under* National events, effect on Illinois
Panic of 1893, *see under* National events, effect on Illinois
Parades (mid-1800s), **9**:215–17 memorial for Grant, **174**:35–39 political (1884), **174**:33–35
Parks, **16**:98–99, map *98*; **33**:index; **34**:index; **102**:99–100, list 99
Peace pipes, *see* Calumets
Peacock, Elijah, **99**:80

31

38

Author-Title
Key

Appropriate grade levels are given in parentheses.

1 Alcock, Gudrun. *Run, Westy, Run.* (4–6)
2 Alcock, Gudrun. *Turn The Next Corner.* (5–8)
3 Allen, Merritt P. *The Wilderness Way.* (7–9)
4 Anderson, Anita M. *Wild Bill Hickok.* (5–9)
5 Anderson, Betty B. *Powder Monkey.* (6–9)
6 Andrist, Ralph K. *Steamboats on the Mississippi.* (6–9)
7 Aulaire, Ingri d', and Edgar d' Aulaire. *Abraham Lincoln.* (K–5)
8 Ayars, James. *The Illinois River.* (7 up)
9 Bailey, Bernadine. *Abe Lincoln's Other Mother: The Story of Sarah Bush Lincoln.* (6–12)
10 Bailey, Bernadine. *Abraham Lincoln: Man of Courage.* (4–6)
11 Bailey, Bernadine. *Picture Book of Illinois.* (4–5)
12 Baker, Elizabeth. *Fire in the Wind.* (5–8)
13 Baker, Nina Brown. *Big Catalogue: The Life of Aaron Montgomery Ward.* (5–8)
14 Baker, Nina Brown. *The Story of Abraham Lincoln.* (4–6)
15 Bare, Margaret A. *John Deere: Blacksmith Boy.* (3–5)
16 Bartlett, Mabel, and John E. Grinnell. *Illinois: Know Your State.* (7–12)

17 Beals, Frank. *Chief Black Hawk.* (4–7)
18 Beckhard, Arthur. *Black Hawk.* (7 up)
19 Benary-Isbert, Margot. *The Long Way Home.* (7–10)
20 Benét, Laura. *Famous Poets for Young People.* (6–10)
21 Bentel, Pearl. *Co-ed off Campus.* (7–10)
22 Biemiller, Ruth. *Dance: The Story of Katherine Dunham.* (6–10)
23 Blassingame, Wyatt. *They Rode the Frontier.* (7 up)
24 Borland, Kathryn K., and Helen R. Speicher. *Allan Pinkerton: Young Detective.* (3–5)
25 Bowman, James. *Mike Fink.* (5–12)
26 Bragdon, Lillian. *Abraham Lincoln: Courageous Leader.* (4–5)
27 Britt, Albert. *An America That Was.* (7 up)
28 Buchheimer, Naomi. *Let's Go Down the Mississippi with La Salle.* (4–5)
29 Burt, Olive. *Brigham Young.* (7–12)
30 Burt, Olive. *Wind before the Dawn.* (6–9)
31 Burtschi, Mary. *Vandalia: Wilderness Capital of Lincoln's Land.* (7 up)
32 Carmer, Carl. *America Sings: Stories and Songs of Our Country's Growing.* (5–9)
33 Carpenter, Allan. *Illinois from Its Glorious Past to the Present.* (5–9)
34 Carpenter, Allan. *Illinois: Land of Lincoln.* (8 up)
35 Cary, Barbara. *Meet Abraham Lincoln.* (2–5)
36 Cavanah, Frances. *Abe Lincoln Gets His Chance.* (3–5)
37 Cleven, Cathrine. *Black Hawk: Young Sauk Warrior.* (3–5)
38 Coatsworth, Elizabeth. *The Last Fort.* (7 up)
39 Colver, Anne. *Abraham Lincoln: For the People.* (2–4)
40 Cooke, David C. *Fighting Indians of America.* (6 up)
41 Crane, Florence. *Gypsy Secret.* (7–10)
42 Craz, Albert. *Getting to Know the Mississippi River.* (4–7)
43 Daugherty, James. *Abraham Lincoln.* (6 up)
44 de Leeuw, Adèle. *George Rogers Clark: Frontier Fighter.* (3–6)
45 Derleth, August. *Father Marquette and the Great Rivers.* (5–9)

46 Dobler, Lavinia and Edgar A. Toppin. *Pioneers and Patriots: The Lives of Six Negroes of the Revolutionary Era.* (6–9)

47 Du Jardin, Rosamond. *Young and Fair.* (7–9)

48 Eifert, Virginia. *Three Rivers South: The Story of Young Abe Lincoln.* (6 up)

49 Eifert, Virginia. *With a Task before Me: Abraham Lincoln Leaves Springfield.* (7 up)

50 Emery, Anne. *Tradition.* (7–12)

51 Erwin, Betty. *Behind the Magic Line.* (5–7)

52 Faber, Doris. *Clarence Darrow: Defender of the People.* (5–7)

53 Faber, Doris. *Enrico Fermi: Atomic Pioneer.* (5–9)

54 Felton, Harold. *Mike Fink: Best of the Keelboatmen.* (5 up)

55 Fermi, Laura. *The Story of Atomic Energy.* (6–9)

56 Finlayson, Ann. *Runaway Teen.* (6–9)

57 Fisher, Aileen. *My Cousin Abe.* (7 up)

58 Fleming, Alice. *Doctors in Petticoats.* (7–9)

59 Fleming, Alice. *Great Women Teachers.* (7 up)

60 Forsee, Aylesa. *Frank Lloyd Wright: Rebel in Concrete.* (7 up)

61 Foster, Genevieve. *Abraham Lincoln.* (4–7)

62 Fox, Mary Virginia. *Ambush at Fort Dearborn.* (5–8)

63 Franchere, Ruth. *Hannah Herself.* (7–11)

64 Franchere, Ruth. *The Travels of Colin O'Dae.* (6–9)

65 Frazier, Carl, and Rosalie Frazier. *The Lincoln Country in Pictures.* (4 up)

66 Friermood, Elizabeth. *Head High, Ellen Brody.* (7–12)

67 Garst, Shannon, and Warren Garst. *Wild Bill Hickok.* (6 up)

68 Gies, Joseph. *Wonders of the Modern World.* (9 up)

69 Gilbert, Miriam. *Jane Addams: World Neighbor.* (4–6)

70 Graham, Alberta. *La Salle: River Explorer.* (4–6)

71 Graham, Shirley. *Jean Baptiste Pointe De Sable: Founder of Chicago.* (7–10)

72 Grant, Bruce. *American Forts Yesterday and Today.* (6 up)

73 Grant, Bruce. *Northwest Campaign: The George Rogers Clark Expedition.* (7–11)

74   Grant, Madeleine. *Alice Hamilton: Pioneer Doctor in Industrial Medicine.* (7 up)

75   Gridley, Marion. *Indian Legends of American Scenes.* (5–9)

76   Gurko, Miriam. *Clarence Darrow.* (8 up)

77   Havighurst, Walter, ed. *Midwest and Great Plains.* (5–8)

78   Hawkinson, John. *Our Wonderful Wayside.* (3–5)

79   Hays, Wilma. *Pontiac: Lion in the Forest.* (5–8)

80   Heagney, Anne. *De Tonti of the Iron Hand and the Exploration of the Mississippi.* (6–9)

81   Heagney, H. J. *Chaplain in Gray—Abram Ryan: Poet-Priest of the Confederacy.* (7–10)

82   Heaps, Willard. *Riots, U.S.A. 1765–1965.* (8 up)

83   Heiderstadt, Dorothy. *Indian Friends and Foes.* (6–9)

84   Hiller, Carl. *From Tepees to Towers.* (8 up)

85   Holbrook, Stewart. *Wild Bill Hickok Tames the West.* (4–7)

86   Hollmann, Clide. *Pontiac, King of the Great Lakes.* (7–12)

87   Horgan, Paul. *Citizen of New Salem.* (8 up)

88   Horn, Madeline. *The New Home.* (4–6)

89   Hunt, Irene. *Across Five Aprils.* (6 up)

90   Hunt, Mabel Leigh. *Better Known as Johnny Appleseed.* (7 up)

91   Jagendorf, M. A. *Sand in the Bag and Other Folk Stories of Ohio, Indiana, and Illinois.* (6–9)

92   Jones, Helen. *Over the Mormon Trail.* (4–6)

93   Judson, Clara. *Abraham Lincoln: Friend of the People.* (5–8)

94   Judson, Clara. *City Neighbor: The Story of Jane Addams.* (6–8)

95   Judson, Clara. *The Green Ginger Jar.* (6–8)

96   Judson, Clara. *The Lost Violin: They Came from Bohemia.* (5–7)

97   Judson, Clara. *Reaper Man: The Story of Cyrus Hall McCormick.* (5–10)

98   Judson, Clara. *St. Lawrence Seaway.* (5–9)

99   Kelly, Regina. *Chicago: Big-Shouldered City.* (7–10)

100   Kelly, Regina. *Lincoln and Douglas: The Years of Decision.* (5–8)

101   Kelly, Regina. *Marquette and Joliet.* (5–8)

102 Kilduff, Dorrell, and C. H. Pygman. *Illinois: History, Government, Geography.* (6–12)

103 King, Martha. *The Key to Chicago.* (5–9)

104 Kjelgaard, Jim. *The Coming of the Mormons.* (5–9)

105 Kjelgaard, Jim. *The Explorations of Père Marquette.* (6–9)

106 Koral, Bella. *Abraham Lincoln.* (2–5)

107 Latham, Frank. *Abraham Lincoln.* (7 up)

108 Lauber, Patricia. *Changing the Face of North America: The Challenge of the St. Lawrence Seaway.* (5–8)

109 Lauber, Patricia. *The Mississippi: Giant at Work.* (4–7)

110 Lavine, Sigmund. *Allan Pinkerton: America's First Private Eye.* (7 up)

111 Lavine, Sigmund. *Famous Merchants.* (6–9)

112 Lawson, Marion. *Proud Warrior: The Story of Black Hawk.* (5–8)

113 Lawson, Robert. *The Great Wheel.* (6–9)

114 Leavitt, Jerome. *America and Its Indians.* (5–9)

115 Lenski, Lois. *Houseboat Girl.* (4–6)

116 Lent, Henry. *Men at Work in the Great Lakes States.* (5–8)

117 McCague, James. *Flatboat Days on Frontier Rivers.* (4–6)

118 McCague, James. *Mississippi Steamboat Days.* (4–5)

119 McCall, Edith. *Forts in the Wilderness.* (4–7)

120 McCall, Edith. *Men on Iron Horses.* (4–7)

121 McGovern, Ann. . . . *if you grew up with Abraham Lincoln.* (1–4)

122 McKown, Robin. *Heroic Nurses.* (8 up)

123 McNeer, May. *America's Abraham Lincoln.* (5–10)

124 McNeer, May. *Armed with Courage.* (5–8)

125 McNeer, May. *Give Me Freedom.* (6–9)

126 McNicol, Jacqueline. *Elizabeth for Lincoln.* (4–5)

127 Martin, Patricia. *Abraham Lincoln.* (2–5)

128 Mason, Miriam. *Frances Willard: Girl Crusader.* (3–5)

129 Meadowcroft, Enid. *Abraham Lincoln.* (5–8)

130 Meadowcroft, Enid. *By Secret Railway.* (4–7)

131 Meredith, Robert, and E. Brooks Smith, eds. *Exploring the Great River: Early Voyagers on the Mississippi from De Soto to La Salle.* (7 up)

132 Meyer, Edith. *Champions of the Four Freedoms.* (7 up)

133 Miers, Earl Schenck. *Abraham Lincoln in Peace and War.* (6–9)

134 Miers, Earl Schenck. *That Lincoln Boy.* (5–8)

135 Miller, Helen. *George Rogers Clark: Frontier Fighter.* (4–6)

136 Mooney, Elizabeth. *Jane Addams.* (5–8)

137 Myers, Elisabeth. *George Pullman: Young Sleeping Car Builder.* (3–5)

138 Myron, Robert. *Shadow of the Hawk: Saga of the Mound Builders.* (6 up)

139 Naden, Corinne. *The Chicago Fire, 1871: The Blaze That Nearly Destroyed a City.* (6–9)

140 Nathan, Adele, and W. C. Baker. *Famous Railroad Stations of the World.* (5–9)

141 Nathan, Adele. *Seven Brave Companions.* (4–8)

142 Nathan, Dorothy. *Women of Courage.* (6–9)

143 Neyhart, Louise. *Giant of the Yards.* (6–10)

144 Neyhart, Louise. *Henry's Lincoln.* (3–6)

145 Noble, Iris. *Clarence Darrow: Defense Attorney.* (7 up)

146 Noble, Iris. *Labor's Advocate: Eugene V. Debs.* (8 up)

147 Nolan, Jeannette. *Abraham Lincoln.* (6 up)

148 Nolan, Jeannette. *The Gay Poet: The Story of Eugene Field.* (7 up)

149 Nolan, Jeannette. *George Rogers Clark: Soldier and Hero.* (6 up)

150 Nolan, Jeannette. *La Salle and the Grand Enterprise.* (6–9)

151 Nolan, Jeannette. *The Little Giant: Stephen A. Douglas.* (6–9)

152 Nolan, Jeannette. *The Story of Ulysses S. Grant.* (4–7)

153 Nolan, Jeannette. *The Victory Drum.* (4–7)

154 North, Sterling. *Abe Lincoln: Log Cabin to White House.* (5 up)

155 Orrmont, Arthur. *Master Detective: Allan Pinkerton.* (7–12)

156 Peithmann, Irvin. *Indians of Southern Illinois.* (7 up)

157 Perl, Lila. *Red-Flannel Hash and Shoo-fly Pie: American Regional Foods and Festivals.* (7 up)

158 Peterson, Harold. *Forts in America.* (5 up)

159 Peterson, Helen. *Jane Addams: Pioneer of Hull House.* (2–4)

160 Place, Marian. *John Wesley Powell: Canyon's Conqueror.* (5–7)

161 Pliss, Louise. *The Strange Journey of Kippy Brooks.* (3–5)

162 Potter, Marian. *Copperfield Summer.* (5–7)

163 Randall, Ruth. *I Mary, A Biography of the Girl Who Married Lincoln.* (7 up)

164 Randall, Ruth. *Lincoln's Animal Friends.* (5–8)

165 Rátz, Margaret. *Exploring Chicago.* (4–6)

166 Rauch, Mabel. *The Little Hellion.* (6–9)

167 Rauch, Mabel. *Vinnie and the Flag-Tree: A Novel of the Civil War in Southern Illinois—America's Egypt.* (8–10)

168 Ray, Bert. *We Live in the City.* (1–2)

169 Raymond, Charles. *The Trouble with Gus.* (6–9)

170 Raymond, Charles. *Up from Appalachia.* (6–10)

171 Redway, Maurine, and Dorothy Bracken. *Marks of Lincoln on Our Land.* (6 up)

172 Roesch, Roberta. *World's Fairs: Yesterday, Today, Tomorrow.* (5–9)

173 Rosenheim, Lucile. *Kathie: The New Teacher.* (6–10)

174 Sandburg, Carl. *Prairie-Town Boy.* (7 up)

175 Sattley, Helen. *Annie.* (6–9)

176 Selvin, David. *Champions of Labor.* (8 up)

177 Selvin, David. *Eugene Debs: Rebel, Labor Leader, Prophet.* (8 up)

178 Severn, Bill. *Adlai Stevenson: Citizen of the World.* (8 up)

179 Silverberg, Robert. *Bridges.* (6–9)

180 Simon, Charlie May. *Lays of the New Land.* (7 up)

181 Smith, Eunice. [The Jennifer Books]
    181a *The Jennifer Wish.* (4–6)
    181b *The Jennifer Gift.* (4–6)
    181c *The Jennifer Prize.* (4–6)
    181d *Jennifer Is Eleven.* (5–6)
    181e *Jennifer Dances.* (5–7)
    181f *High Heels for Jennifer.* (6–8)

182 Smith, Fredrika. *Wilderness Adventure.* (5–8)

183 Smucker, Barbara. *Wigwam in the City.* (4–7)

184 Stanek, Muriel. *You and Chicago.* (4–6)

185 Syme, Ronald. *La Salle of the Mississippi.* (6–9)

186 Taylor, Florance. *Jim Long-Knife.* (5–8)

187 Vance, Marguerite. *The Lamp Lighters: Women in the Hall of Fame.* (8–12)

188 Veglahn, Nancy. *Peter Cartwright: Pioneer Circuit Rider.* (8 up)

189 Wagoner, Jean. *Jane Addams: Little Lame Girl.* (3–5)

190 Ward, Martha. *Adlai Stevenson: Young Ambassador.* (3–5)

191 Weaver, John. *Tad Lincoln: Mischief-Maker in the White House.* (6–10)

192 Wernecke, Herbert. *Tales of Christmas from Near and Far.* (5–7)

193 Werstein, Irving. *Labor's Defiant Lady: The Story of Mother Jones.* (7 up)

194 Whitney, Phyllis. *A Long Time Coming.* (6–10)

195 Whitney, Phyllis. *Willow Hill.* (7–10)

196 Wibberley, Leonard. *Wes Powell: Conqueror of the Grand Canyon.* (7 up)

197 Wise, Winifred. *Jane Addams of Hull House.* (7–10)

198 Young, Ben T. *Rock River Ranger.* (6–9)

199 Zehnpfennig, Gladys. *Carl Sandburg: Poet and Patriot.* (8 up)

200 Ziegler, Elsie. *Light a Little Lamp.* (7–9)

Annotated
Bibliography

Each entry in this Annotated Bibliography begins with bibliographic details, including purchasing information where necessary. No prices are given since these are subject to frequent change. If the illustrator of a book is well known, he is named; otherwise the citation merely indicates that the book is illustrated. Grade levels are given in parentheses. A book is entirely or almost entirely about Illinois if no page references appear in the citation. When page references are given, these indicate the pages which include Illinois information and such additional material necessary to make that information clear. This same wide range of pages is also used in the Subject Index entries. The abbreviation "Fic" identifies fiction. A few books on the list are out of print. For each of these the symbol "OP" appears at the end of the citation. Although an out-of-print book no longer can be purchased from the publisher, it may be available in a local library or through interlibrary loan.

1   **Alcock, Gudrun.** *Run, Westy, Run.* Lothrop, 1966. 158p. (4–6) Fic
This straightforward, realistic story of the experience of a Chicago boy whose truancy and waywardness land him in a detention home has valuable food for thought for both young

and old on present-day problems of city boys and girls. The story appeal is strong enough to attract not only intermediate-grade readers but also reluctant junior-high readers.

2 **Alcock, Gudrun.** *Turn the Next Corner.* Lothrop, 1969. 160p. (5–8) Fic

Twelve-year-old Ritchie finds it difficult enough suddenly to have to live in a small apartment and to have his mother at work all day. But hearing his respected lawyer father rightfully called a "jailbird" is almost more than he can bear. Ritchie's adjustment to these new circumstances is slowly accomplished through the friendship of a courageous crippled boy. In spite of only fair writing, the author succeeds in portraying well a boy's gradually coming to understand the point of view of young people of a different social and ethnic status. Details relating to the Joliet penitentiary and to the crowded and turbulent conditions of blacks and whites in Chicago's Near North Side are vivid and thought-provoking.

3 **Allen, Merritt P.** *The Wilderness Way.* McKay, 1954. 246p. (7–9) p.81–186

Filled with danger, heroism, and intrigue, this highly fictionalized account of La Salle's journeys is primarily an exciting adventure story. Laurent Delair lends the appeal of a boy hero, and the voyageur Joe Yon provides the fun. In spite of the fictional element, the book authentically portrays the life and character of the voyageurs and the unique qualities of La Salle and Tonti, who recognized the vastness of the territory drained by the Mississippi River and the importance of the region to France.

4 **Anderson, Anita M.** *Wild Bill Hickok.* Harper (American Adventure Series), 1960. 251p. illus. (5–9) p.1–15, 164–75

This biography is useful in working with reluctant readers because of its upper-grade subject interest and its intermediate-grade reading level. The Illinois material is limited, but Troy Grove boys and girls will be proud to find a book that tells of Wild Bill Hickok's early years in their vicinity, and all Illinois boys and girls will be proud that he belongs to their state.

5 **Anderson, Betty B.** *Powder Monkey.* New York Graphic
Society, 1962. 196p. (6–9) p.30–55, 61–67, 89–103, 147–51.

There is danger and excitement in this story of a Galena
boy who serves as a Union powder monkey in the important
Tennessee and Mississippi River battles. Since the setting of one-
fourth of the book is in Cairo or at the Cairo wharf, the author
has an opportunity to acquaint readers with several significant
contributions of Illinois people to the Civil War. The navy yard,
the army prison camp, the army hospital, and Camp Darling
(all at Cairo), and a number of Illinois officers appear in the
story. Two good maps trace movements out of Cairo into strategic battles.

6 **Andrist, Ralph K.** *Steamboats on the Mississippi.* American Heritage (American Heritage Junior Library), 1962.
153p. illus. (6–9) p.97–99, 104–7, 125, 138–39

Although there is little in this book specifically on Illinois,
much of the material (discussed without definite location) about
the Mississippi's banks, boats, rivermen, lore, and the like, is as
true of Illinois' western boundary as of any other portion of the
upper Mississippi. Made up of a variety of interesting episodes,
sketches, and descriptions, and illustrated with numerous large
and small colored and black-and-white pictures, the book provides enjoyable desultory reading and useful information. Index.

7 **Aulaire, Ingri d', and Edgar d' Aulaire.** *Abraham Lincoln.*
Illus. by authors. Doubleday, 1957. unpaged. (K–5)
p.23–46

The life of Lincoln has undoubtedly never been published
in so attractive and artistic a picture book. Both the beautiful
stone lithographs and the well-written narrative trace the story
of his life rapidly but coherently from the time of his birth to
the peace after the Civil War. The author-artists have expertly
selected those incidents which would most interest young children and have sensibly soft-pedaled or omitted unfortunate incidents; for example, the assassination is not mentioned. The
reading text covers what would amount to about thirty pages.
The end-sheet map is helpful.

8 **Ayars, James.** *The Illinois River.* Holt, 1968. 182p. illus.
(7 up)

This much-needed book begins with an explanation of the
formation of the land in Illinois (which explains "how the river
came to be") and of the findings regarding the prehistoric inhabitants of Illinois. This is followed by a chronological presentation of the important events taking place in the Illinois River
Valley from the beginning of Illinois history to the present. It
includes a particularly good presentation of the explorations of
Marquette and Joliet and of La Salle, and a very just and sympathetic account of the Indians of Illinois. This history and the
succeeding discussions of the "harnessing" and uses of the river
give excellent information about the riverbed and its course,
kinds of boats and their uses, cargoes, passenger service, canals,
locks, river towns, the Illinois Waterway, problems connected
with the river, wildlife, park and conservation areas. The author
has succeeded in giving much useful information; he has also
made clear the great importance of the river in the development
of the state. Index.

9 **Bailey, Bernadine.** *Abe Lincoln's Other Mother: The Story
of Sarah Bush Lincoln.* Illus. by Howard Simon. Messner,
1941. 227p. (6–12) p.173–223.

The book begins with the coming of Sarah Bush Lincoln
to the Lincoln cabin in Indiana and ends with Lincoln's visit to
his stepmother just before he leaves for Washington. The relationship between the two is perhaps idealized, but boys and girls
are made aware of the great influence upon Lincoln of the person
who best understood him in his impressionable years. There is
accurate information about the Thomas Lincoln family and
about the pioneer hardships in the state thirty years before the
Civil War.

10 **Bailey, Bernadine.** *Abraham Lincoln: Man of Courage.*
Houghton (Piper Books), 1960. 191p. illus. (4–6) p.53–159.

Here is probably the most readable of the easy biographies
of Lincoln. Miss Bailey tells the story of his life from his eighth
year through his death. Although the book is only moderately

fictionalized, it is enlivened by an unusual number of anecdotes, many of which are not ordinarily found in so short an account. The numerous full-page drawings, washed in bright blue, are not particularly attractive, but they do depict many details of the period. Maps. Chronology.

11 **Bailey, Bernadine.** *Picture Book of Illinois.* Whitman (The United States Books), 1964. 30p. (4–5).

This quick survey of Illinois includes a short history of the state, a commentary on the topography, and brief discussions of the products of farms, mines, oil wells, and quarries. Mention is made of a number of large towns and cities and of outstanding people. A third of the book is devoted to Chicago—its history, industries, colleges, attractions, and famous citizens. Every double-page spread has an illustration, color alternating with black and white. In the study of Illinois, the book can serve well as an introduction or a summary. Map. Index.

12 **Baker, Elizabeth.** *Fire in the Wind.* Houghton, 1961. 244p. illus. (5–8) Fic

A good impression of the vigorous spirit of the rapidly growing city and many details of life in Chicago in 1871 are worthwhile phases of this book. The plot is obviously contrived and in many places moves slowly, but it does include a number of exciting adventures. Eleven-year-old Jeff, whose father is a detective with the Chicago police department, becomes involved in a series of unlikely, dangerous undertakings in an attempt to clear a friend who has been accused of stealing a valuable horse and important papers. He returns home just in time to help his father save their house during the great Chicago fire. The last two chapters are devoted to the fire.

13 **Baker, Nina Brown.** *Big Catalogue: The Life of Aaron Montgomery Ward.* Harcourt, 1956. 115p. illus. (5–8) p.59–115 OP

This rags-to-riches story is far more acceptable than an old Alger tale because it is true. The improbable Alger "breaks" are replaced with hard work and only a likely amount of luck; in place of a puppet hero there is fairly good characterization;

and instead of the making-money motive there is the serving-others ideal. The book shows the development of an outstanding Chicago business and gives glimpses of such important Chicago events as the great fire and the Columbian Exposition. One of its most unusual contributions is the account of the founding and early history of the National Grange.

14 Baker, Nina Brown. *The Story of Abraham Lincoln.* Grosset, 1952. 176p. illus. (4–6) p.76–142

This book, which begins with Lincoln at the age of seven and ends with his death, moves at a fast pace, contains much conversation, and is easy enough reading for fourth graders. They will be able to understand the very brief and simple explanations of the problems of slavery, secession, and the war. However, the book may be long for average fourth-grade readers. Its best use is for reluctant readers in the upper grades. Its meager treatment, or complete omission, of some of the significant national issues with which Lincoln was connected, its lack of dates, and its presentations of certain doubtful points as truths limit its usefulness.

15 Bare, Margaret A. *John Deere: Blacksmith Boy.* Bobbs, (Childhood of Famous Americans), 1964. 200p. illus. (3–5) p.165–92

One-fourth of the space of this better than average Childhood of Famous Americans book is devoted to the adult years of John Deere. The author does especially well in showing how Deere's natural bent for improving machines and his experience as a blacksmith prepare him for his tremendous success in developing and manufacturing a workable steel plow. Furthermore, she makes clear why such a plow was so desperately needed by Illinois farmers and gives an account of Deere's working on the problem in early Grand Detour and Moline.

16 Bartlett, Mabel, and John E. Grinnell. *Illinois: Know Your State.* Southern Illinois Univ. Pr. (Carbondale, 62901), 1964. 103p. illus. (7–12)

Considering the lack of good informational books on Illinois, this book is worth having in spite of its paper binding and its text-workbook features. It presents the significant facts about the state's geography, history, government and constitution, culture, economy, natural resources and their conservation, and citizens who have made important contributions. The state constitution, good maps, and diagrams are included.

17 **Beals, Frank.** *Chief Black Hawk.* Harper (The American Adventure Series), 1961. 252p. illus. (4–7)

This is the story of the Sauk chief, Black Hawk, from the time he was made a brave until his death in 1838. Decidedly idealized, he is presented as courageous, gentle, very fair to both white men and Indians. Keokuk, his enemy, is put in a reasonably good light—differing in opinion with Black Hawk in that he believed the Indians should obey the white men and move west across the Mississippi. The choppy, unattractive style is the result of deliberate simplification for problem readers. To further carry out this purpose there are questions at the ends of the chapters and a word list at the end of the book.

18 **Beckhard, Arthur.** *Black Hawk.* Messner, 1957. 192p. (7 up) p.9–175

Beckhard makes the controversial Black Hawk a great hero —courageous in the face of injustice to his people and as fearless in battle as he was reluctant to take life unnecessarily. In his unsuccessful efforts to unite the Indian tribes for protection against the white men, he is presented as a great leader with the abilities of a general and the ideals of a peacemaker. The book gives a good description of life in the large Indian village of Saukenuk, repeatedly throws light upon the unfair treaty into which the Indians were tricked at Saint Louis in 1804, and includes a rather detailed account of the Black Hawk War. All are presented with complete sympathy for the Indians. Indian personalities well known in Illinois in the early 1800s and several important military figures move in and out of the book. Index.

19 **Benary-Isbert, Margot.** *The Long Way Home.* Harcourt, 1959. 280p. (7–10) p.113–59 Fic

This is a well-written moving story of Christoph, an East

German lad seeking refuge with an American GI who had befriended him during World War II. It portrays the life of a foreign family whose members work hard to manage a small restaurant in Chicago's Loop and relates the experiences of a foreign boy in a Chicago school. There are good descriptive details of a number of places and areas in and around Chicago. Since it is written by a German woman new to Chicago, her descriptions of the impressions this city makes upon a foreigner are sympathetic and real.

20 Benét, Laura. *Famous Poets for Young People.* Dodd, 1964. 160p. photos. (6–10) p.85, 87–88, 104–12, 148–51

Illinois lays some claim to three of the twenty-six poets appearing in this collection—Eugene Field, Vachel Lindsay, Carl Sandburg. Comments on the major works of each are included in the sketch of his life. Since Lindsay and Sandburg were born and grew up in Illinois and Field spent his last twelve years as a columnist on the *Chicago Daily News*, Illinois serves as background to a part of each of these three short biographies.

21 Bentel, Pearl. *Co-Ed off Campus.* McKay, 1965. 182p. (7–10) Fic

This teen-age novel, which gives the impressions of a college student during her cadet training in a Chicago settlement house, presents a good picture of a present-day underprivileged south-side Chicago neighborhood and the typical services offered by an inner-city welfare center. In spite of rather ordinary writing, the book can be absorbing reading for boys as well as for girls, since there is a sympathetic account of a boy to whom exciting gang activities are beginning to seem far more inviting than repeated unpleasant home experiences.

22 Biemiller, Ruth. *Dance: The Story of Katherine Dunham.* Doubleday, 1969. 144p. photos. (6–10) p.11–93, 115–19, 140–44

The life of the famous dancer from her early childhood in a Chicago ghetto to her more recent past as Artist in Residence at Southern Illinois University makes an adequate fictionalized biography. Despite poverty, her father's opposition to her chosen career, and racial prejudice, Miss Dunham succeeded in becoming one of the most original dancers of this century, an outstanding choreographer, and a successful research anthropologist in many parts of the world. The author manages to include a good deal of the way of life of struggling Negro theatre people in Chicago and of poor Negroes in Joliet.

23 **Blassingame, Wyatt.** *They Rode the Frontier.* Watts, 1959. 182p. (7 up) p.4–25, 63–82 OP
Covering a period from the late seventeenth century to the present, *They Rode the Frontier* gives the account of fifteen zealous, courageous, frontier preachers. Illinois material appears in only the chapters on Marquette and Peter Cartwright, but information on Cartwright for the grades is so scarce as to justify the purchase of this book. Index.

24 **Borland, Kathryn K., and Helen R. Speicher.** *Allan Pinkerton: Young Detective.* Bobbs (Childhood of Famous Americans), 1962. 200p. illus. (3–5) p.147–67
A greater proportion of the book is devoted to the adult life of Allan Pinkerton than is usually accorded the subjects of the simple biographies in this series. There are interesting details of his childhood in Scotland, followed by the story of how, as a young man in Dundee, Illinois, he accidentally came to be a detective, and later, in Chicago, to establish his own famous detective agency.

25 **Bowman, James.** *Mike Fink.* Illus. by Leonard Fisher. Little, 1957. 145p. (5–12) p.49–50, 65–68, 86–109
According to the rivermen, Mike Fink, greatest of them all, controlled the Ohio and Mississippi Rivers from Pittsburgh to New Orleans in the days of the keelboats. The tales of his exploits are among the best of the American tall tales—filled with adventure, courage, skill, and fun. His keelboat and the activities on it were typical of what might be seen from any spot on the Ohio and Mississippi River banks of Illinois. The fearsome rivalry between keelboat men and paddle-wheel and steamboat men is also an exciting part of Illinois history. Most pertinent

to Illinois literature are the rousing tales of Mike and the Cave-in-Rock pirates.

26 Bragdon, Lillian. *Abraham Lincoln: Courageous Leader.* Abingdon (Makers of America), 1960. 125p. illus. (4–5) p.38–88

Almost without anecdote and completely unfictionalized, this simple biography gives the main facts of Lincoln's life from birth to death. Although the presentation is rather cold, it impresses the reader with Lincoln's sincerity and with his determination to save the Union. Uninspired writing makes the book inferior to Genevieve Foster's Lincoln biography, which most intermediate-grade boys and girls can read. Bragdon's biography would be used in preference to Foster's only where somewhat easier reading and slightly more Civil War material are desired. Large print.

27 Britt, Albert. *An America That Was.* Barre Pubs. (South St., Barre, Mass. 01005), 1964. 196p. illus. (7 up)

As the author indicates on the title page, the purpose of this book is to tell "what life was like on an Illinois farm seventy years ago." From firsthand experience and in fascinating detail he recalls the old, but changing, ways regarding family relationships, houses, food, work, play, school, reading, religion, manners, morals, and speech during the late 1800s. Fitted skillfully into these discussions there is plentiful information about the natural aspects of rural western Illinois—its topography, trees, flowers, animals. The book can be made entertaining and worthwhile to boys and girls if only small portions are recommended at appropriate times and with evident intent.

28 Buchheimer, Naomi. *Let's Go Down the Mississippi with La Salle.* Putnam (Let's Go Series), 1962. 48p. illus. (4–5) p.14–24

This account of La Salle's expedition down the Mississippi is made interesting by details of encounters with Indians and by the sustained feeling of adventure which comes from risking the dangers of the unknown. The book is easy enough for young readers and exciting enough for reluctant readers beyond the grades indicated above. Map. Glossary.

29 **Burt, Olive.** *Brigham Young.* Messner, 1956. 192p. (7–12) p.58–63, 70–92, 111–13

Beginning with his boyhood and ending with his death, this biography of Brigham Young describes his unswerving and untiring efforts to establish Mormonism. The mighty force of his faith carries him, almost joyously, through missionary service in England, persecution in Missouri and Illinois, and the successful organization of a trek to Utah for thousands of his followers. The part of the book which takes place in Nauvoo is especially useful, for there is little material available for boys and girls about that city. Index.

30 **Burt, Olive.** *Wind before the Dawn.* Day (Daughters of Valor), 1964. 189p. (6–9) p.11–64 Fic

With the good sense and strength of a mature adult, Katherine Hustin, a real teen-age Mormon, cares for her dying parents at the time the Mormons are forced out of Nauvoo, and after their death drives a wagon in the trek from Nauvoo to Utah. From Council Bluffs on she takes full charge of three motherless children. The story, which is packed with danger and hardship, gives an excellent description of life in the amazing town of Nauvoo in the early 1840s and a moving account of the persecution and departure of the Mormons. The personalities of a number of their leaders are exceptionally well portrayed in the book.

31 **Burtschi, Mary.** *Vandalia: Wilderness Capital of Lincoln's Land.* Huston-Patterson Corp. (Decatur, Ill. 62521), 1963. 158p. illus. (7 up) OP

Vandalia: Wilderness Capital of Lincoln's Land begins with the early development of the second state capital of Illinois and proceeds to bring out much subsequent history through biographical material about seven Illinois governors, Abraham Lincoln, and many other persons important in the Vandalia area in the first part of the nineteenth century. Descriptions of original buildings and places, of valuable historical writings, and of contemporary art expressions of the past show the town as a rewarding place to visit. Considerable space is given to the past literary activity of the region as well as to the history. This adult book is packed with interesting anecdotes and facts, but it is not likely to be read in toto even by adults. It would be very useful in the hands of a wise teacher who would guide pupils' reading to specific portions pertinent to current assignments. Index.

32 **Carmer, Carl.** *America Sings: Stories and Songs of Our Country's Growing.* Knopf, 1962. 243p. illus. (5–9) p.84–91

One of these twenty-nine folk tales and one of these twenty-nine folk songs belong to Illinois. The tale of Mike Fink tells of his attempt to jump across the Mississippi River from Cairo to Birds Point. In addition to being fun, it may well give the young reader an idea of the interesting geographical setting of Cairo. The song "Shawnee Town" will require an explanation of "bushwacking," a method commonly used by boatmen along the banks of the rivers bordering Illinois to propel their boats upstream. (Music given for each song.)

33 **Carpenter, Allan.** *Illinois from Its Glorious Past to the Present.* Childrens Press, 1963. 93p. illus. (5–9) OP

This cursory treatment presents many aspects of Illinois—geography, history, resources, occupations, products, people. The facts are packed in too closely to be remembered, but the book does bring out clearly the succession of important steps in the growth of the state and gives interesting bits of legend and lore. It would therefore serve either as an overall introduction to the study of Illinois or as a quick summary. A chronology and lists of miscellaneous facts, important people, and places to visit are useful. Index. Maps.

34 **Carpenter, Allan.** *Illinois: Land of Lincoln.* Childrens Press, 1968. 207p. illus. (8 up)

A large part of the book is devoted to the historical aspects of Illinois—the history of the state from prehistoric times to the present, of towns and cities important at various periods, of labor, education, and religion. There is information about outstanding citizens in politics, business, science, philanthropy, athletics, social work, and the arts. There are rather detailed discussions of peoples, government, resources, transportation, manufacturing, agriculture, forests, wildlife, and interesting tourist attractions in various parts of the state. Transitions between subjects are often lacking, and facts and statistics are so numerous that use of the very good index is absolutely imperative. Attractive format, an excellent table of contents, a chronology, about 100 illustrations (photographs and reproductions), over twenty maps, and several charts are valuable features. Index.

35 **Cary, Barbara.** *Meet Abraham Lincoln.* Random (Step-Up Books), 1965. 86p. illus. (2–5) p.30–63

This simple story of Lincoln's life, with its easy vocabulary, extremely short sentences, and large print, is third-grade reading material. But the inclusion of important events and issues of the period, explained briefly and clearly, will help a slow reader in the upper grades in his study of the United States and should contribute to his appreciation of history.

36 **Cavanah, Frances.** *Abe Lincoln Gets His Chance.* Rand, 1959. 92p. illus. (3–5) p.74–92

This biography moves rapidly over the life of Abraham Lincoln from his birth through his parting from his stepmother before his departure for Washington. Although the book has no distinction, it would serve well as a stepping stone between the Augusta Stevenson biography and the somewhat more difficult but far better written ones by Genevieve Foster, Clara Ingram Judson, and May McNeer (nos. 61, 93, and 123 respectively in this list). It has simplicity of style and interesting anecdotes and detail, and avoids wisely and skillfully such biographical problems as the Ann Rutledge romance and Mary Lincoln's disposition.

37 **Cleven, Cathrine.** *Black Hawk: Young Sauk Warrior.* Bobbs (Childhood of Famous Americans), 1966. 200p. illus. (3–5) Almost entire book

Following the usual pattern of the series, this biography

tells the story of the boyhood of Black Hawk and briefly points out the main events of his adult years. Throughout he is portrayed as a courageous leader, seeking only the just rights of the Sauks, his people, against the unfair and cruel intrusion of white men. Details regarding the way of life of the Illinois Indians in the early nineteenth century will be helpful when younger children or older reluctant readers are studying Illinois. Chronology.

38 **Coatsworth, Elizabeth.** *The Last Fort.* Illus. by Edward Shenton. Holt, 1952. 250p. (7 up) p.170, 192–248 Fic OP

After the British capture Quebec during the French and Indian War, Alexis Picard, French-Canadian lad, is sent by his father from Quebec to find a home for the family in the Fort Chartres region. The story is permeated by the French settlers' hatred of the English and dread of British encroachment. Less than half the book has an Illinois background, but it portrays excellently the way of life of the French and the Indians in the Fort Chartres and Cahokia region. Although the valuable descriptions slow up the action, there are numerous exciting incidents. A good map of the route of the voyageurs and one of the Cahokia-Kaskaskia area are included.

39 **Colver, Anne.** *Abraham Lincoln: For the People.* Garrard (A Discovery Book), 1960. 76p. illus. (2–4) p.27–58

Beginning in his eighth year, this easy-reading book tells the story of Lincoln through his death. In spite of the choppy style, the author succeeds, through conversation and anecdote, in making facts interesting and characters come alive. The book will therefore serve both as a practice reading book and an introductory information book on Lincoln. It is regrettable that there are slight inaccuracies in a few details.

40 **Cooke, David C.** *Fighting Indians of America.* Dodd, 1966. Part I, 226p., Part II, 206p. photos. (6 up) Part II, p.52–53, 148–63

This book is a combination of two of the author's earlier books, *Fighting Indians of the West* (1954) and *Indians on the Warpath* (1957). Only the account of Pontiac's death and the story of Black Hawk (both in *Indians on the Warpath*) are part of Illinois history. The portrayal of Black Hawk's character, the explanation of the circumstances which led up to the Black Hawk War, and the report of the main events of the war are presented with complete sympathy for the Indians.

41 Crane, Florence. *Gypsy Secret.* Random, 1957. 245p. (7–10) Fic OP

Randy, a sixteen-year-old gypsy girl, is purposely left in the gypsy camping ground in Calhoun County when her people return to Chicago. Her unhappiness is gradually overcome by the kindness of the people with whom she lives and a wholesome romance with a neighbor lad. Good characterization, mystery, and romance make this story attractive to older girls. The book gives a glimpse of gypsy tenement life in Chicago, a description of the Calhoun County apple festival, and a good idea of the Calhoun County countryside. The glossary of gypsy words and phrases is interesting in general and helpful in reading the book.

42 Craz, Albert. *Getting to Know the Mississippi River.* Coward, 1965. 64p. illus. (4–7) Scattered pages

Very little of this up-to-date book deals specifically with the miles of river that bound Illinois, but over one-third of the text is devoted to matters which pertain to nearly all of the river. A general survey of the geography and history of the Mississippi Valley is followed by outstandingly lucid descriptions of the various kinds of boats used on the river in the past and present. There are good discussions of river control and of the consequent increase in industry, traffic, and recreational facilities. One of the best features of the book is the excellent manner in which special river terms are made clear as they are used. Index.

43 Daugherty, James. *Abraham Lincoln.* Illus. by the author. Viking, 1943. 216p. (6 up) p.26–105

From the point of view of writing, this is one of the best biographies of Lincoln for older boys and girls. The style is masculine, impressive, and vital. With Walt Whitman's frankness and Lincoln's own power and simplicity, Daugherty has portrayed the mental and spiritual side of Illinois' greatest man. The author has paid young people the compliment of being able to sense Lincoln's pathetic aloneness in his greatness; he has given them credit for caring about more than external actions by emphasizing Lincoln's logical thinking, his passion for justice, his recognition of true worth even in the crudest and roughest people. This is a book that should be read aloud with young people that they may listen to the poetic phrasing and the apt, graphic wording. The book itself is beautiful. The thirty-four full-page and six half-page lithographs are done in shades of brown, with soft tonal effects but strong composition. Index.

44 de Leeuw, Adèle. *George Rogers Clark: Frontier Fighter.* Garrard (A Discovery Book), 1967. 80p. illus. (3–6) p.45–69
The portion of this biography which deals with Clark in Illinois tells of his taking the British-controlled fort at Kaskaskia and the village of Cahokia without bloodshed, of his making friends with the French settlers and the Indians, and of his famous march from Kaskaskia to Vincennes. The story, which covers his life from his thirteenth year to his old age, is authentic and fast-moving, but the style is pedestrian because the vocabulary and sentences are planned for third-grade reading ability. Its best use would be with older reluctant readers.

45 Derleth, August. *Father Marquette and the Great Rivers.* Farrar (Vision Books), 1955. 188p. illus. (5–9) p.101–27, 155–61, 171–85 OP
This biography, which covers Marquette's life from the time he landed in Quebec until his death, makes Marquette appear decidedly the more important of the two leaders of the Joliet-Marquette expedition. There is good information about Indian customs and about the Mississippi Valley. Tenets of the Catholic faith appear naturally. The maps, a feature lacking in the Nathan biography (no. 141 in this list), do not add much to this book.

46 Dobler, Lavinia, and Edgar A. Toppin. *Pioneers and Patriots: The Lives of Six Negroes of the Revolutionary Era.* Doubleday, 1965. 118p. illus. (6–9) p.18–29

Since material about Jean Baptiste Pointe du Sable (one of the pioneers included in this collection) is very difficult to find, and since Du Sable is recognized as the founder of Chicago, this book is worthwhile in the study of Illinois. The straightforward presentation is limited to the characteristics of the man and the main facts known about his life.

47 Du Jardin, Rosamond. *Young and Fair.* Lippincott, 1963. 187p. (7–9) Fic

Much information about life in Chicago in the 1880s is woven into a love story of a lonely department-store clerk and the son of the wealthy owner. Details of the Chicago fire, of boardinghouse life, of amusements, clothing, customs, and places are naturally and accurately revealed. Despite many coincidences and pat solutions, the book will be popular with girls, for it presents interests and problems of today's girls in a time setting that is fascinatingly different.

48 Eifert, Virginia. *Three Rivers South: The Story of Young Abe Lincoln.* Dodd, 1953. 176p. illus. (6 up) p.1–90 Fic

The three rivers are the Sangamon, Illinois, and Mississippi, upon which Abraham Lincoln, transporting produce, made his second flatboat trip to New Orleans. Although fictionalized, the story includes real Illinois people and places and actual occurrences in Lincoln's life. Whereas most other writers using Lincoln material point up his fine qualities through description, Mrs. Eifert reveals his initiative, resourcefulness, and leadership through exciting incidents. It is unfortunate that the artistic, full-page drawings are not always placed and identified satisfactorily in relation to the text.

49 Eifert, Virginia. *With a Task before Me: Abraham Lincoln Leaves Springfield.* Illus. by Manning De V. Lee. Dodd, 1958. 217p. (7 up) Fic OP

With a Task before Me begins with Lincoln as a captain in the Black Hawk War in 1832 and describes his life during the years when he was storekeeper, postmaster, and surveyor in New Salem, legislator in Vandalia, and lawyer in Springfield. The findings of the author's research regarding Lincoln and Ann Rutledge, Mary Owen, and Mary Todd are woven into an absorbing narrative to which the account of the controversy over the Rebecca letters and Shield's ensuing duel with Lincoln add zest. In addition to a good presentation of Lincoln's personality, character, and principles, the book has value for accurate details of daily life in the frontier village of New Salem and a glimpse of society life in the growing town of Springfield.

50   Emery, Anne. *Tradition.*   Vanguard, 1946. 250p. (7–12)
Fic

Stacy Kennedy, a senior during World War II in a large Chicago suburban high school, struggles between loyalty to the village tradition of proudly associating with only the "old" families and loyalty to the more truly American ideals of active brotherhood. She chooses the latter, and helps Dorothy and Charlie Okamoto, fine young people of Japanese descent, make a happy adjustment to the school. The book has the usual appeals of high-school language, bickerings, dates, sports. More importantly, it faces sensibly and squarely a race situation likely to be a problem today in any large high school.

51   Erwin, Betty. *Behind the Magic Line.*   Little, 1969. 178p.
illus. (5–7) p.3–137 Fic

Sensitive, enthusiastic, imaginative Dozie, one of ten children, longs for the beauty, friendship, and freedom her two-room home in the poverty-stricken, predominantly Negro section of Chicago cannot give her. Only when her older brother gets into trouble and the family flees the city, does she begin to find her dreams coming true. The plot is logically worked out, the characters sympathetically presented, and the setting vividly pictured. Not only are the desperate want and limited opportunities in a Chicago slum area made impressive but the fineness, orderliness, and pride of many of the people living there are so well portrayed as to give young readers a fairer understanding of these people than they have received from news media.

52 Faber, Doris. *Clarence Darrow: Defender of the People.*
Illus. by Paul Frame. Prentice, 1965. 72p. (5–7) p.26–50, 72

Covering the time from his thirteenth year through his death, this brief biography includes important facts about Darrow as a member of the city legal department of Chicago and later as a lawyer for the Chicago and Northwestern Railway. It discusses clearly several of the very famous trials in which Darrow served as defense lawyer—one of which, the trial concerning the Pullman strike, took place in Illinois. In these discussions the author gives a good idea of Darrow's extreme financial ups and downs, personal traits, and variety of interests. The book furnishes good material for upper-grade reluctant readers.

53 Faber, Doris. *Enrico Fermi: Atomic Pioneer.* Prentice, 1966. 86p. illus. (5–9) p.57–61, 76–86

This brief story of Fermi from his twelfth year to his death stresses particularly his scientific interests and accomplishments. It includes a good account of Fermi's famous experiment at the University of Chicago (which resulted in the first successful nuclear chain reaction) and of his later preparations for work on peacetime uses of the atom.

54 Felton, Harold. *Mike Fink: Best of the Keelboatmen.* Dodd, 1960. 159p. (5 up) p.76–87

This retelling of the exploits of the famous riverman has the same zest and humor that are found in James Bowman's *Mike Fink* (no. 25 in this list), but uses a simpler vocabulary and shorter episodes.

55 Fermi, Laura. *The Story of Atomic Energy.* Random (World Landmark Books), 1961. 184p. photos. (6–9) p.80–91, 111–12, 149–50

This is the history of the atom, from the ideas of the early Greek philosophers to the successful operations of reactors in the twentieth century. The high point of the long, slow development took place at the University of Chicago in 1942 under the direction of Enrico Fermi. The detailed account of Fermi's famous experiment furnishes information about an important event in modern science to which Illinois made a contribution. Index.

56 Finlayson, Ann. *Runaway Teen.* Doubleday, 1963. 143p. (6–9) Fic

The bigness and coldness of Chicago and the desperate monotony of factory life are impressed upon the reader through the experiences of sixteen-year-old Libby, who has run away from home to be on her own. The circumstances which draw her temporarily into a group of young hoodlums give a good picture of adolescent gang life. The information about Chicago is incidental and limited but accurate.

57 Fisher, Aileen. *My Cousin Abe.* Nelson, 1962. 282p. (7 up) p.195–282

This is a unique portrayal of Abraham Lincoln in that it presents him as he appeared to his relatives. Dennis Hanks, the cousin who lived in the Lincoln home when Abe was growing up and who accompanied the Lincoln family to Illinois, tells Abe's story with sincerity, affection, and pride. Intimate and entertaining incidents make this book especially appealing to young people. The language of Dennis Hanks was the Kentucky dialect. By merely suggesting this, the author has made the book easier to read than if it were in full dialect, but she has at the same time maintained the flavor and attractiveness of Hanks' speech. The book is rich in important and less important details about Illinois.

58 Fleming, Alice. *Doctors in Petticoats.* Lippincott (Cadmus Edition), 1964. 159p. (7–9) p.70–85

Only one of these well-written accounts of ten women doctors furnishes any Illinois material, namely, that of Dr. Alice Hamilton. This brief biography makes a very readable summary of Madeleine Grant's *Alice Hamilton: Pioneer Doctor in Industrial Medicine* (*see* no. 74 in this list).

59 Fleming, Alice. *Great Women Teachers.* Lippincott, 1965. 157p. (7 up) p.101–14

Except for the brief comment on page 68 telling of Alice Freeman Palmer's becoming dean of women at the University of Chicago, only the life story of Ella Flagg Young concerns readers interested in Illinois. The story reveals not only the contributions to education of this famous superintendent of the Chicago public schools, but also the status and problems of the development of public school education in Illinois in the second decade of the twentieth century. The other nine stories of inspired women teachers would furnish excellent recruitment and career guidance material.

60 **Forsee, Aylesa.** *Frank Lloyd Wright: Rebel in Concrete.* Macrae, 1959. 181p. photos. (7 up) p.18–67

In spite of the book's being largely devoted to Wright's startling and controversial ideas and theories of architecture, the chief events of his personal life from early childhood to death and his character are adequately and sensibly handled. For the adolescent reader interested in architecture, there is helpful and inspiring material. For those studying Illinois, there is information about the planning and construction of a number of unusual Illinois buildings and about several famous architects, such as Daniel H. Burnham and Louis Sullivan. Four of the twenty beautiful photographs in the book illustrate Wright's achievements in Illinois. Index.

61 **Foster, Genevieve.** *Abraham Lincoln.* Scribner (Initial Biography), 1950. 111p. illus. (4–7) p.39–77

Genevieve Foster's well-written biography of Lincoln is one of the best for boys and girls because it gives each outstanding event of Lincoln's life from birth to death in its right proportion and relative significance. Though the story is short, every character comes alive and every incident rings true. Most fourth-graders can read it and enjoy it, but its subject matter and dignity of approach will hold the interest of upper-grade readers. The many green-and-white illustrations also appeal to a wide age range.

62 **Fox, Mary Virginia.** *Ambush at Fort Dearborn.* St. Martins, 1962. 173p. illus. (5–8) Fic

Fourteen-year-old Tom Malen (many of whose descendants still live in Chicago) comes with his family to Fort Dearborn. Soon after they have established a home a few miles from the fort, Tom is captured by the Senecas. The account of his life with them, his friendship with another captive (a Potawatomi lad), and his escape from the camp and from the Fort Dearborn massacre, is filled with accurate details of pioneer and Indian life, true events, and real people of the early 1800s. The plot has enough momentum to hold interest, but the author loses more than one opportunity to make a dangerous incident exciting.

63 Franchere, Ruth. *Hannah Herself.* Crowell, 1964. 176p. (7–11) Fic

Soon after their marriage in 1827, Ellen and Jonathan Stewart attempt to establish an unwanted academy near present-day Beardstown. Ellen's sister, Hannah, sixteen, who comes from the East for an extended visit, is unable to understand Ellen's willingness to give up the luxuries of her home in the East for the hardships of pioneer life. But Hannah, too, is soon caught up in Jonathan's crusade to "combat ignorance." Her romantic interest in a student who is aiding runaway slaves, and Ellen's and Jonathan's hope that she will encourage the son of the wealthy man who could endow the academy, lend a fillip to the story. The book has excellent background material on education, transportation, housing, customs, and daily life typical of an Illinois pioneer settlement.

64 Franchere, Ruth. *The Travels of Colin O'Dae.* Illus. by Lorence Bjorklund. Crowell, 1966. 261p. (6–9) Fic

In the 1830s fourteen-year-old Colin leaves Chicago and his canal-digger father to join a troupe of traveling players. They cut across country to the Illinois, set up a crude showboat, and perform at river towns from Hennepin to St. Louis. Exhausting work, stage fright, and maneuvering an unwieldy boat in fog and storms are only a few of the harrowing experiences which turn Colin into an able, self-assured youth. In addition to a good story, the book gives details of the lives of the poverty-stricken Irish immigrants in Chicago, of the river-town people along the Illinois, and of a typical showboat family in the days of the country's financial difficulties under Andrew Jackson.

65 Frazier, Carl, and Rosalie Frazier. *The Lincoln Country in Pictures.* Hastings, 1963. 96p. photos. (4 up) p.19–96
These one hundred and five good photographs with brief accompanying comments for each depict Lincoln and his environment from his birth to his departure from Springfield. Since some sixty of the ninety pictures in Illinois are exteriors and interiors at restored New Salem, they make clear to twentieth-century boys and girls many unfamiliar objects used by Illinois pioneers. The book should inspire children and their parents to visit New Salem and other Lincoln shrines. Unfortunately the specific locations of Lincoln statues and the names of sculptors are not given.

66 Friermood, Elizabeth. *Head High, Ellen Brody.* Doubleday, 1958. 240p. (7–12) p.140–65, 219–27 OP
Seventeen-year-old Ellen Brody, having grown up at the turn of the century in the bleak poverty of the factory section of an Indiana industrial town, resolves she will use her talent in art to get her family into an environment of comfort. But the arrival of an understanding, dynamic young man, who establishes a successful settlement house to help the entire neighborhood, results in Ellen's complete change of interests. Her consequent visits to Chicago give the author an opportunity to present accurate descriptions of the work at Hull House, of life in a home of wealth, and of the horrors of the famous Iroquois Theater fire.

67 Garst, Shannon, and Warren Garst. *Wild Bill Hickok.* Messner, 1952. 183p. (6 up) p.1–16, 130–32
This is a well-told story of Wild Bill Hickok from his twelfth year until his death. Only a small portion of the book is set in Illinois, but it is worth including in this bibliography because of the pride Illinois boys have in the fact that Wild Bill Hickok was a native of their state. Moreover, the book includes a good picture of farm life in northern Illinois during

the 1840s and '50s, a discussion of the state's participation in the Underground Railroad, and a glimpse of early Troy Grove. Index.

68 **Gies, Joseph.** *Wonders of the Modern World.* Crowell, 1966. 241p. photos. (9 up) p.82–101

Among the thirteen marvelous achievements in engineering described here in detail is that of Chicago's reversing a river's course to solve the city's obstinate problem of water pollution. The solution to this problem, engineers found, was complete purification, a solution from which every major city can benefit. The story of combining a lake and three rivers to furnish a water supply and a sewage system for a great metropolitan area is fascinating because it is the story of how one seemingly insurmountable difficulty after another is overcome. Map. Index.

69 **Gilbert, Miriam.** *Jane Addams: World Neighbor.* Abingdon (Makers of America), 1960. 128p. illus. (4–6)

This satisfactory, simple account of the life of Jane Addams from her childhood in Cedarville through her death in Chicago brings out clearly her personality and achievements. The development of Hull House and the beginnings of other Chicago social welfare agencies in which Jane Addams had a part are well presented. Glimpses of prominent people who worked with her are brief, but they do make the reader aware of her influence upon social, political, and industrial leaders between the years 1880 and 1935. The book will appeal chiefly to girls too young to enjoy Judson's *City Neighbor.*

70 **Graham, Alberta.** *La Salle: River Explorer.* Abingdon (Makers of America), 1954. 128p. illus. (4–6) p.63–110

Most of this clearly written biography is devoted to La Salle's preparations for exploring and fortifying the Mississippi River Valley, but it includes enough detail of early Illinois to be of value in the study of the state. The short, choppy sentences result in a style that is poor but easy enough for fourth grade. The author misses many opportunities for heightening interest through dramatic incident. Map.

71

71 **Graham, Shirley.** *Jean Baptiste Pointe De Sable: Founder of Chicago.* Messner, 1953. 180p. (7–10) p.47–167

Of this biography of De Sable, a black man who could not prove he was a free Negro, and who later became a founder of Chicago, the author says, "My book is not accurate history nor is it pure fiction. It is an imaginative interpretation of all the known facts in a sincere attempt to create a reasonable and plausible whole of essential truth." Regardless of the "imaginative interpretation," the book does give an excellent idea of the foresight of De Sable in recognizing the strategic location of the Chicago area for a great city and of his genuine efforts to maintain peace between Indians and white inhabitants. His fine character and attractive personality are well drawn. Few books bring out so sharply and fairly the white man's injustices to the Indians. There are notes on source materials and a helpful introduction. Index.

72 **Grant, Bruce.** *American Forts Yesterday and Today.* Illus. by Lorence Bjorklund. Dutton, 1965. 381p. (6 up) p.174–78

With a map for each of eight regions, the book comments briefly, state by state, on the location and history of the more than 1200 forts in our fifty states. It includes only four pages devoted to the seventeen forts of Illinois, but the material included is important in the study of Illinois history and difficult to find elsewhere in so clear a presentation. Glossary of terms. Index.

73 **Grant, Bruce.** *Northwest Campaign: The George Rogers Clark Expedition.* Putnam, 1963. 185p. illus. (7–11) p.31–125, 173–77

The trip made by Clark and his Big Knives from Kentucky to Kaskaskia, their clever capture of Fort Gage without firing a shot, their making allies of the French and Indians in the town and environs, their almost superhuman march to Vincennes, and their seizure of Fort Sackville are recounted in this highly fictionalized, stirring biography. Clark is portrayed as an attractive young leader of prodigious strength and courage, unusual military skill, and outstanding ability to analyze and get along with people. Conditions in Illinois during the Revolution and the state's part in that conflict are well presented.

74 **Grant, Madeleine.** *Alice Hamilton: Pioneer Doctor in Industrial Medicine.* Abelard, 1967. 223p. photos. (7 up) p.15–21, 50–100, 182–87

This substantial, well-written biography of Dr. Alice Hamilton covers her life from birth to old age. Soon after completing her training, she came to teach in the Woman's Medical School of Northwestern University. Almost immediately she became a social worker at Hull House, which she regarded as home for twenty years. Because of her successful investigation of working conditions in the white lead industries, Governor Deneen made her director of his commission to study industrial diseases in Illinois, a commission which was responsible for legislation protecting workers from dust and fumes. After several years of conducting research for the Federal Government in the hazardous occupations, she became professor of industrial medicine at Harvard. She is distinguished as a pioneer in efforts to protect the health and safety of American workers. Index.

75 **Gridley, Marion.** *Indian Legends of American Scenes.* Donohue (711 S. Dearborn, Chicago 60605), 1939. 127p. illus. (5–9) p.43–45

Although there is only one story specifically about Illinois in the forty-seven from twenty-six states and Canada, the book is worth including in an Illinois unit of study. A page of introduction to the one story explains what groups of Indians made up the Illinois Confederacy, and what causes contributed to their extinction. That story, "Starved Rock," gives a fine portrayal of the famous Indian Pontiac and a definite impression of his importance. The narrative itself is interesting and relates a well-known incident in the history of Illinois.

76 **Gurko, Miriam.** *Clarence Darrow.* Crowell, 1965. 280p. (8 up) p.37–84, 90–106, 111–27, 147–50, 181–86, 191–206, 264–66

This full-length story of the life of Clarence Darrow gives an accurate portrayal of his fine personality and character, follows clearly the growth of his political and social ideals, and emphasizes his valuable contributions to the development of labor negotiation and criminal law. Included are excellent accounts of famous trials, such as those connected with the Haymarket riot, the Pullman strike, and the Loeb-Leopold case, in which Darrow figured prominently and which are important events in Illinois history. Index.

77 **Havighurst, Walter, ed.** *Midwest and Great Plains.* Fideler (United States Social Studies), 1967. photos. (5–8) p.204–17 and scattered pages OP

In the first four parts of this supplementary textbook, the land and climate, history, people, and means of earning a living are discussed for both the Midwest and the Great Plains. The material which is applicable to Illinois is plentiful in this general treatment. Pages 204–17 are exclusively devoted to the state, and provide information in detail about its land and climate, natural resources, products, industries, and larger cities. Among the many photos in the book, over twenty were taken in Illinois. Maps. Charts. Index.

78 **Hawkinson, John.** *Our Wonderful Wayside.* Illus. by the author. Whitman, 1966. unpaged. (3–5)

This delightful book is bound to develop both creativity and love of nature in a child. For each season, except winter, there are brief descriptions of a few common wild fruits, plants, birds, and animals. Simple directions for making jam, baskets, and pictures enhance the enjoyment of the wayside. Charming illustrations clarify these descriptions and directions. Aids to the recognition of such dangers as poison ivy and nettles are slipped in skillfully. Although no mention is made of Illinois, everything in the book is typical of this state. Since the author's home is in Chicago, it may well be concluded that it is the Illinois wayside he describes.

79 **Hays, Wilma.** *Pontiac: Lion in the Forest.* Houghton (Piper Books), 1965. 189p. illus. (5–8) p.155–59, 170–82

Pontiac, leader of forty-seven tribes, spent his life in Ohio. Nevertheless, he holds a place of some importance in Illinois history because he was constantly stirring up the Illinois tribes in an effort to enlist their cooperation against the encroaching white men. In this easy, full-length biography may be found the accounts of two visits made by Pontiac to the Cahokia area— one in which he unsuccessfully sought guns and troops and one in which he purportedly met his death at the hands of an Illinois Indian. The author relates the latter event as if it were fact and then, in a note at the end of the book, comments on the uncertainty of the place and circumstances of Pontiac's death.

80 **Heagney, Anne.** *De Tonti of the Iron Hand and the Exploration of the Mississippi.* Kenedy (American Background Books), 1959. 190p. illus. (6–9) p.49–54, 122 OP

Beginning with De Tonti at Fort Joseph in 1681 and ending with his death in 1704, this fictionalized account presents his dangerous explorations of the Mississippi Valley, his brave defense of French colonists and friendly Indians, and his devoted loyalty to his frequently absent leader, La Salle. For more than twenty years during this period De Tonti, though often away, was in command of Fort St. Louis, the fort on Starved Rock. Ordinary as the writing may be, the book gives information about the building of the fort, the relationship between the French and Indians of the area, the successful fur trade, and the important part played by the Jesuits who accompanied the explorers. Index.

81 **Heagney, H. J.** *Chaplain in Gray—Abram Ryan: Poet-Priest of the Confederacy.* Kenedy (American Background Books), 1958. 190p. illus. (7–10) p.132–33, 141–55 OP

This book should be carefully examined before it is used in the classroom. The writing is strained, sentimental, and at points stilted; the subject over-idealized. In spite of generous and courageous help given both Protestant and Catholic soldiers by Father Abram Ryan, the dominance of one faith may open the book to criticism for public school use. It is included in this list because it explains the Knights of the Golden Circle, an organization of some size in Illinois during Civil War days.

82 **Heaps, Willard.** *Riots, U.S.A. 1765–1965.* Seabury, 1966. 186p. (8 up) p.84–97, 108–17

Two of the thirteen major riots discussed in this book took place in Illinois—the Pullman strike of 1894 and the East St. Louis race riot of 1917. Each of the two accounts begins with the causes of the trouble, follows the successive steps chronologically (using exact dates, places, and names of real people involved), and concludes with a brief summary of the immediate results. The presentations are clear and unprejudiced. Index.

83 **Heiderstadt, Dorothy.** *Indian Friends and Foes.* McKay, 1958. 130p. illus. (6–9) p.54–62

Among the thirteen Indian leaders included in this book, only Black Hawk lived in Illinois. His story, briefly told, gives the main events of his life and indicates his importance in Illinois history. The author portrays Black Hawk as fierce and savage, and his rival, Keokuk, as peaceloving and friendly. She calls attention to the huge statue of Black Hawk by Lorado Taft, which stands near Oregon, Illinois, overlooking the Rock River Valley. Index.

84 **Hiller, Carl.** *From Tepees to Towers: A Photographic History of American Architecture.* Little, 1967. 106p. photos. (8 up) p.48, 51, 53, 55–57, 66–67, 80–81

Over one hundred lovely photographs with accompanying text trace the development of architecture in America from its beginnings among the Indians to the present. This chronological survey includes buildings for various purposes—in the author's words, "shelter for living, for worship, for government, for learning, for business, for amusement." Influences resulting in different types of architecture and the contributions of a number of outstanding architects are included. An excellent, illustrated glossary adds much to the usefulness of the book. General index. Index of architects.

85 **Holbrook, Stewart.** *Wild Bill Hickok Tames the West.* Random (Landmark Books), 1952. 178p. illus. (4–7) p.3–23

This biography tells the story of James Hickok (Wild Bill)

from the age of ten through his death at the hands of Broken-Nose-Jack McCall, who, incidentally, was also an Illinois man. Filled with incident after incident of excitement, bravery, shooting, and killing in the untamed West, it would please any adventure-loving teen-age boy. Yet its reading level is scarcely above fourth grade. Though meager, the Illinois material is of double worth in that it makes clear the part the state played in the Underground Railroad and gives satisfying details of the Illinois boyhood of a famous hero of the West.

86 **Hollmann, Clide.** *Pontiac, King of the Great Lakes.* Hastings, 1968. 151p. illus. (7–12) p.82, 108, 117–26, 128, 131–34

Pontiac was the one Indian chief who, in the 1760s, attempted to unite all Indian tribes of the Midwest into a confederacy and, thereby, succeeded at times in carrying on effective resistance to the domination of the British. This book gives no evidence that the Illinois Indians aided Pontiac, but it does comment on their fear and jealousy of him. It tells of a useless trip he made to the Fort Chartres area to get help in his plans for war and of a second visit to accept an invitation to participate in the *Dance-of-Chiefs*. The account of this second visit gives details of his being killed by an Illinois Indian—a version of Pontiac's death which has not been authenticated. This biography, better written and more thorough than the one by Hays (no. 79 in this list), brings out exceptionally well Pontiac's ability to persuade with fine oratory, to plan skillful strategy, and to lead in peace and war. Map. Index.

87 **Horgan, Paul.** *Citizen of New Salem.* Illus. by Douglas Gorsline. Farrar, 1961. 90p. (8 up)

In July 1831, the twenty-two-year-old Lincoln settled in the pioneer village of New Salem. Horgan tells the true story of the following six years, when, through his own efforts and the understanding and generosity of friends, Lincoln overcomes the handicaps of poverty, ungainliness, lack of education, and repeated disappointments. Excellently written, the book is an appreciative analysis of Lincoln's maturing, mentally, socially, culturally, and emotionally. It was in New Salem that Lincoln showed promise of the fine courage, sense of justice, sympathetic concern for the rights of the individual, and magnanimity of spirit that eventually made him great. The book is a mine of information on everyday pioneer life—homes, furniture, food, clothing, work, play, sicknesses and their treatment, costs—all against the dangerous and beautiful backdrop of virgin wilderness.

88 **Horn, Madeline.** *The New Home.* Illus. by Harve Stein. Scribner, 1962. 128p. (4–6) Fic

Undersized twelve-year-old Andrew, one of five children in an Illinois pioneer family, tries repeatedly and unsuccessfully to do something worthy of a grown man. He finds satisfaction when he performs a useful and dangerous feat and learns that "small folks" can do some things "big folks" cannot. The details of everyday indoor and outdoor pioneer living and of many of the usual pioneer dangers and adventures are vividly woven into an interesting narrative. The style is undistinguished but easy and acceptable. The entire story takes place twelve miles southeast of Watseka.

89 **Hunt, Irene.** *Across Five Aprils.* Follett, 1964. 223p. (6 up) Fic

In an exceptionally moving and well-written Civil War story the author presents the hardship, suffering, and courage of a young farm boy near Newton, Illinois, as he takes full responsibility for the farm work all too heavy for his years. The tragic home situations resulting from conflicting opinions and divided loyalties among brothers and neighbors are brought vividly to life against the authentic background of the national struggle in which they participated. Depending upon research, family records, and her grandfather's memories, the author has thoroughly verified her impressive story.

90 **Hunt, Mabel Leigh.** *Better Known as Johnny Appleseed.* Lippincott, 1950. 209p. (7 up) p.126, 162–76, 198

Undoubtedly the real Johnny Appleseed, John Chapman, spent most of his life in Ohio and Indiana, but there is evidence that he tramped the prairies and planted apple seeds in Illinois as well. This is a fictionalized account of Chapman's life from birth to death, interspersed with numerous anecdotes, which, although they may not always be authentic, do enliven the heavier portions of the book and reveal clearly the nature of his character. The few pages with an Illinois setting present unusually well both the bleak loneliness of the treeless prairie as experienced by the early settlers and the genuine help and hope given them by Johnny Appleseed. Map.

91 Jagendorf, M. A. *Sand in the Bag and Other Folk Stories of Ohio, Indiana, and Illinois.* Vanguard, 1952. 184p. (6–9) p.135–84

Thirteen of the stories in this collection are from Illinois, including the title story. They belong to different locations from Cairo to Chicago, and, at times, mention actual place names and real people. Packed with fun, feats of strength, and cleverness, these brief, homely, vigorous folk tales are good reading for older boys and girls.

92 Jones, Helen. *Over the Mormon Trail.* Childrens Press (Frontiers of America Series), 1963. 127p. illus. (4–6) p.9–14, 26–31

The early pages of this book give a good idea of the beauty and progressiveness of Nauvoo, the largest town in Illinois in the 1840s, and of the great difficulties the inhabitants experienced at the hands of their neighbors. Most of the book is devoted to the extreme hardships of the Mormons as they made their way by various means to the Salt Lake Valley. The only justification for including in this list a book so poorly written and so limited in Illinois material is that it does contain information about Nauvoo which is unavailable elsewhere for intermediate grades. Map.

93 Judson, Clara. *Abraham Lincoln: Friend of the People.* Follett, 1950. 206p. illus. (5–8) p.57–162

Although fictionalized sufficiently to hold the interest of boys and girls, this excellent biography of Lincoln is based solidly upon facts. Through narrative and a bit of description it brings Lincoln to life with all his awkwardness, straightforwardness, genuineness, kindness, and fairness. Lincoln's family and friends are well portrayed in proper perspective. In addition to facts pertaining to the characters and events of Lincoln's life, the book is valuable for the wise selection of parts quoted from Lincoln's speeches and for the emphasis upon mid-century political events in Illinois. The endsheet map contributes to the usefulness of the book; the fourteen Kodachromes picturing the Chicago Historical Society Lincoln dioramas, and a number of pen drawings by Robert Frankenstein add to both its attractiveness and its worth.

94 **Judson, Clara.** *City Neighbor: The Story of Jane Addams.*
Scribner, 1951. 130p. illus. (6–8)
This story of Jane Addams from the age of six to seventy dwells briefly on her childhood and emphasizes particularly her founding of Hull House and her successful supervision of that settlement house for forty years. Her understanding of the needs of the immigrant and her remarkable ability to guide the inexperienced philanthropist are well brought out. There are glimpses of late nineteenth-century Freeport, Rockford College, and Hull House and environs. A number of Chicagoans prominent in social work at the turn of the century appear in the book.

95 **Judson, Clara.** *The Green Ginger Jar.* Houghton, 1949.
211p. illus. (6–8) Fic
The Green Ginger Jar serves several purposes. No other story for boys and girls so well portrays Chicago's colorful Chinatown of the 1930s. It gives an excellent idea of the traditional relationship of the various members of a Chinese family to each other, and of the struggle of the younger generation to become truly American and yet maintain respect for the attitudes and customs of the older members of the family. It presents any immigrant's problems and at the same time it is an outstandingly good story and an entertaining mystery.

96 **Judson, Clara.** *The Lost Violin: They Came from Bohemia.* Follett, 1958. 204p. illus. (5–7) Fic
In 1892 Anna Kovec, thirteen, comes to Chicago with her

mother, brother, and sister to join her father. On the day of her arrival her beautiful old Mittenwald violin disappears. She learns later that the formula for fine old Bohemian glass had been hidden in the case. The story, a mystery, is chiefly the account of the search for the violin. It gives a good picture not only of the Bohemian settlement in the area of Seventeenth Street and Blue Island Avenue but also of the way the Bohemians kept their old traditions and customs and at the same time became good American citizens. The book includes some details of the preparation for the Columbian Exposition of 1893.

97 **Judson, Clara.** *Reaper Man: The Story of Cyrus Hall McCormick.* Follett, 1948. 156p. illus. (5–10) p.93–94, 97–110, 123–29, 133–56

This story of McCormick is also the story of the development of the reaping machine and of the McCormick Manufacturing Company. There is information about the formation of the International Harvester Company, the growth of agricultural implement manufacturing in Illinois, and the beginning of the improvement of labor conditions. Of more general interest are the glimpses of important people, events, and way of life in Chicago in the middle of the nineteenth century.

98 **Judson, Clara.** *St. Lawrence Seaway.* Follett, New rev. ed., 1964. 160p. illus. (5–9) Scattered pages

The author traces the history of this gigantic waterway from its geological origins through years of exploration, canal and lock building, and twentieth-century engineering feats to its completion as a seaway in the 1960s. She gives authentic details of the need for such a waterway, the steps in its construction, the problems involved, and its uses for both navigation and power. The book emphasizes the fine cooperation between Canada and the United States in carrying out the project. Although not much space is devoted to Illinois alone, the impact of the seaway on Chicago as a transportation center and on the industry and economic progress of the state is important to Illinois citizens. Good diagrams, maps, and photographs contribute to the clarity and significance of the book. The lack of an index detracts from its usefulness.

99 Kelly, Regina. *Chicago: Big-Shouldered City.* Reilly, 1962. 158p. illus. (7–10) OP

The author weaves the important events of Chicago's history between 1811 and 1894 into the story of a fictional but typical family. All characters except the members of this family are real people, and they are numerous and important in the city's development. The accounts of Fort Dearborn, Chicago's growth into a town, the nominating convention of 1860, Chicago's part in the Civil War, the great fire of 1871, and the Columbian Exposition are vivid. Details regarding dress, house furnishings, and the arts are especially well presented. The foreword gives a brief history of Chicago from its beginnings to 1812; the epilogue outlines the outstanding work of the Chicago Plan Commission. The book ends with a short historical tour of the city. Not a particularly well written book, nevertheless it is very readable, and the great amount of information is clear and accurate.

100 Kelly, Regina. *Lincoln and Douglas: The Years of Decision.* Random (Landmark Books), 1954. 184p. illus. (5–8) p.30–35, 68–82, 109–70

While pointing up vividly the contrast of character between Abraham Lincoln and Stephen A. Douglas, Regina Kelly makes clear the significant relationship of both to the outstanding national issues of the period. The Missouri Compromise, the Kansas-Nebraska Bill, the organization and early history of the Republican party, and the Dred Scott case are all so simply and clearly presented that an intermediate-grade reader can understand each one and its importance to Illinois as well as to other states. Consequently, although only one-third of the book is set in Illinois, the whole book is a valuable contribution to the understanding of the history of the state in the 1850s and 1860s. Index.

101 Kelly, Regina. *Marquette and Joliet.* Follett, 1965. 144p. illus. (5–8) p.11–13, 55–56, 88–104, 113–18, 134–40

This account of Marquette's and Joliet's discovery and exploration of the Mississippi and Illinois rivers begins with Marquette's first sight of Quebec and ends with the brave priest's death. Since there are details of Marquette's and Joliet's visiting the villages of Illinois Indians on their way down the Mississippi and up the Illinois, and descriptions of the rivers and river banks they passed as they journeyed on the Illinois, Des Plaines, and Chicago rivers, the reader gets a good idea of Illinois in the late 1600s. It is essentially a book of historical information, and yet it has enough danger and excitement to serve as a good adventure story.

102 **Kilduff, Dorrell, and C. H. Pygman.** *Illinois: History, Government, Geography.* Follett, 1962. 208p. illus. (6–12) OP

The well-selected, well-organized information in this textbook is interestingly presented and enriched by over ninety photographs, about twenty-five other illustrations, twenty-five excellent maps, and ten helpful graphs and charts. The material included is basic. After dealing briefly with location, physical features, climate, and natural resources, it traces the state's history from the Mound Builders to the present. As background for the study of Illinois, a short history of the founding of the national government is followed by the complete text and all but the last amendment of the Constitution of the United States, with good explanations interspersed. Discussions of the important federal offices, Congress, cabinet, departments, and agencies follow. In the same way, documents, offices, and branches of the government of Illinois and of local and township governments are presented and explained. Education, farming, products, resources, manufacturing, trade, transportation, cities, and the state's greatest citizens are adequately discussed. Bibliographies, statistical lists, and brief biographies add to the usefulness of the book. Index.

103 **King, Martha.** *The Key to Chicago.* Lippincott (Keys to the Cities Series), 1961. 127p. photos. (5–9)

More attractive in format and more pleasant in style than a guide book, and freer from such teaching devices as questions, charts, and bibliographies than a textbook, this book could well be used for either. The opening chapters are devoted to discussions of Chicago as a seaport and as a city with a wide variety in jobs and industries, in homes and schools, and in recreation and entertainment. The greater portion of the book gives the history of Chicago from the earliest beginnings to the present, treating particularly well the development of her industries and railroads, the contributions of her outstanding industrial and civic leaders, and her plans for the immediate future. No book for boys and girls does better in bringing out the bigness of Chicago in size, in accomplishments, in spending, and in spirit. A good map and thirty photographs and old prints add both usefulness and attractiveness. Index.

104 Kjelgaard, Jim. *The Coming of the Mormons.* Random (Landmark Series), 1953. 183p. illus. (5–9) p.3–42, 60–62

The fourth of this book which deals with the Mormons in Illinois tells of their persecution while in the Nauvoo area and their subsequent evacuation of this town. The Mormons' devotion to their faith and their determination to maintain their religious beliefs are emphasized; their justice toward others and their tolerance of the beliefs of others are evident. A good description of the thriving town of Nauvoo and of the refinement and culture of the Mormons is an important contribution of this book. Index. Maps.

105 Kjelgaard, Jim. *The Explorations of Père Marquette.* Random (Landmark Books), 1951. 181p. illus. (6–9) p.130–48, 163–79

This book tells the story of Marquette from his early days in America to his death. All but two incidents are based upon the actual life of Father Marquette, and those two are typical of Marquette's nature. Only a few of the incidents have actual Illinois settings, but the information presented here about Marquette's explorations is necessary to an understanding of early Illinois history. Characterizations of Marquette and Joliet are fairly good. Very good maps. Index.

106 Koral, Bella. *Abraham Lincoln.* Random, 1952. unpaged. illus. (2–5) p.40–62

Although this large, flat picture book probably could not be read by average primary-grade children, it could be used with them because of the good pictures. Text and illustrations, skimming the life of Lincoln from his birth until his departure from Springfield, bring out the chief aspects of his character and the outstanding events in his life. The pictures are of value for their many details of everyday life in pioneer times.

107 Latham, Frank. *Abraham Lincoln.* Watts (Immortals of History), 1968. 163p. photos. (7 up) p.13–83

The pages indicated above as Illinois material cover Lincoln's years in Illinois and deal almost entirely with the development of his ability to take a successful part in state and national politics. The political issues and problems in which he gradually became interested and for which he eventually had to take responsibility are explained in so clear a fashion that the book would be good supplementary reading for junior and senior high school study of United States history. Many direct and indirect quotations from Lincoln's speeches are a part of these explanations. A number of important Illinois men associated with Lincoln in his political activities are realistically portrayed. Map. Index.

108 Lauber, Patricia. *Changing the Face of North America: The Challenge of the St. Lawrence Seaway.* Coward (Challenge Books), 1959. 96p. photos. (5–8) Scattered pages

This book is concerned with the same material as that found in Judson's *St. Lawrence Seaway* and takes up very nearly the same topics. Emphasis on these topics differs. For example, Lauber puts much less stress upon the historical development and more upon the present limitations and the required improvements for the future uses of the seaway. Furthermore, Lauber's book is both less intensive and less extensive than Judson's, presenting each subject with a simpler approach. Its clear diagrams and maps make it a helpful book. Index.

109 Lauber, Patricia. *The Mississippi: Giant at Work.* Garrard (Rivers of the World), 1961. 95p. photos. (4–7) Scattered pages

The book discusses briefly and simply the source of the river, its course, tributaries, shifts and changes, its usefulness and its dangers from floods, as well as man's efforts to control it. Also presented are the kinds of craft that sail the river. Only a few pages make specific mention of Illinois, but half the text deals with matters of vital concern to the state, and many of the forty photographs could be Illinois scenes. Maps. Index.

110 **Lavine, Sigmund.** *Allan Pinkerton: America's First Private Eye.* Dodd, 1963. 241p. photos. (7 up) p.5–30 and scattered pages

Dangers, excitement, bravery, cleverness, and humor permeate accounts of the procedures used by Pinkerton and his associates to unravel complicated case after case. Although the work of these famous private detectives extended over the entire United States, Illinois places and people figure importantly in the book. For most of Pinkerton's first fifteen years in this country he lived in Dundee, Illinois, working as a cooper for a while; his last twenty-six years were in Chicago. From its establishment in 1850 until Pinkerton's death in 1884, the headquarters of Pinkerton's National Detective Agency were in Chicago. Index.

111 **Lavine, Sigmund.** *Famous Merchants.* Dodd, 1965. 148p. photos. (6–9) p.93–102

Among these dozen success stories only that of Gen. Robert Wood has bearing upon Illinois. Wood originated and brought to fruition the idea of Sears, Roebuck and Company's carrying on a retail department store business in addition to its mail order business. At the time of his retirement in 1954, the company was operating 700 stores. During his regime as president, Allstate Insurance (an international subsidiary of Sears) was founded, the Sears-Roebuck Foundation was organized, Sears' employees' profit-sharing plan was established, and the company expanded into nine Latin American countries. Bits of information about Chicago are included in the few pages dealing with Illinois. Index.

112 **Lawson, Marion.** *Proud Warrior: The Story of Black Hawk.* Hawthorn, 1968. 170p. illus. (5–8) p.11–135

This life of Black Hawk, somewhat fictionalized yet giving a reliable overall impression, follows the famous Sauk warrior's

persistent but failing efforts to stop the encroachment of the
westward-moving white settlers upon his home, Saukenuk. True,
the white man's treatment of the Sauks was shameful, but Black
Hawk and his followers were not quite so blameless nor was
the guilt of their rival, Keokuk, so flagrant as here presented.
Much conversation, action, and danger will please adventure-
loving boys. Readers will learn of the fine qualities of the Sauks
(which are rarely emphasized) and of the Indians' humiliation
at the hands of white men. Index.

113 **Lawson, Robert.** *The Great Wheel.* Illus. by the author.
Viking, 1957. 188p. (6–9) p.51–184 Fic
Little did twelve-year-old Conn dream as Aunt Honora
read his fortune from his tea cup that he really would leave
Ireland, go to America, and "ride the greatest wheel in all the
world." The time arrived when, with Uncle Patrick, he became
an important helper in constructing the great Ferris wheel at
the Columbian Exposition in Chicago. This is a fine story,
crowded with the factual details of the building and use of
the gigantic wheel. There are many satisfactory glimpses of the
fair grounds and buildings and of the famous George Washington Ferris. The black-and-white drawings by the late Robert
Lawson are superb, as always.

114 **Leavitt, Jerome.** *America and Its Indians.* Childrens
Press, 1962. 220p. illus. (5–9) p.202–11
As the author says in his preface, this book "is concerned
with details of the daily lives" of the North American Indians.
Only two of the groups discussed lived in Illinois for any time—
the Ottawa-Potawatomi group in the Chicago area and the
Sauk-Fox group in the northwest part of the state. For each of
these groups there are terse but adequate descriptions of food,
homes, clothes, occupations, tools, transportation, and religion.
The full-page illustrations are of particular worth in the study of
Illinois Indians.

115 **Lenski, Lois.** *Houseboat Girl.* Illus. by the author. Lippincott, 1957. 176p. (4–6) p.1–30 Fic
Although the major portion of this book has to do with

87

the life of a houseboat family on the Mississippi River below the Ohio, the story begins in River City, Illinois. During the early part of the trip down the Ohio River, most of the place names are those of Illinois towns passed or briefly visited. Its value as informational material, however, lies in the fact that the way of life of this family is for the most part typical of the more respectable houseboat families living along the banks of Illinois rivers. Similar material is not available elsewhere. An excellent double-spread map of the lower Ohio and middle Mississippi River valleys adds usefulness to the book.

116 Lent, Henry. *Men at Work in the Great Lakes States.* Putnam, 1958. 128p. photos. (5–8) p.12–15, 100–105

After a brief history of the Great Lakes states, Henry Lent describes twenty-three of their major industries and thereby introduces hundreds of occupations and products common to Ohio, Indiana, Illinois, Michigan, Wisconsin, and Minnesota. Well-organized, interesting subject matter and direct, clear writing, with good photographs and excellent print and page design, make this an attractive information book. Although only two chapters are devoted entirely to Illinois industries (the Union Stockyards in Chicago and the Caterpillar Company in Peoria), the remainder of the book makes excellent background material for the study of Illinois. Index.

117 McCague, James. *Flatboat Days on Frontier Rivers.* Garrard (A How They Lived Book), 1968. 96p. illus. (4–6) p.43–51, 64–68

Good descriptions of flatboats—their construction, uses, cargoes, crews, passengers, and Ohio-Mississippi voyages—include interesting incidents of adventure. Important to the study of Illinois are the accounts of the exciting and dangerous activities in the early Shawneetown and Cave-in-Rock areas around the year 1800. Index.

118 McCague, James. *Mississippi Steamboat Days.* Garrard, 1967. 96p. illus. (4–5)

Good descriptions of various types of steamboats—their structure, uses, crew, types of passengers—comprise the major portion of the text. Colorful accounts of famous accidents and races make the book rather exciting. Although there is almost no specific reference to Illinois, almost all of the information is accurately applicable to the steamboats that plied the waters bordering Illinois. Glossary. Index.

119 McCall, Edith. *Forts in the Wilderness.* Childrens Press (Frontiers of America), 1968. illus. (4–7) p.6–93, 105–21

Forts in the Wilderness deals chiefly with the French forts of Illinois. Tracing their history from 1679 to 1779, the author dwells upon the encounters of La Salle and Tonti with the Illinois Indians, the unsuccessful efforts of Pontiac to enlist the Illinois Indians in his confederacy, and the successful efforts of George Rogers Clark to gain control of the Kaskaskia area for the Americans. This easy fictionalized history is basically accurate and interesting. Map.

120 McCall, Edith. *Men on Iron Horses.* Childrens Press (Frontiers of America), 1960. 125p. illus. (4–7) p.42–56

In simple, informal style, Mrs. McCall makes a lively, readable narrative of the facts pertaining to the arrival of the first little train in Chicago and its first trips out of the city. Names of real people and places give authenticity to the telling.

121 McGovern, Ann. *. . . if you grew up with Abraham Lincoln.* Illus. by Brinton Turkle. Four Winds, 1966. 79p. (1–4) p.46–75

Using the question-and-answer approach, the author describes New Salem in Lincoln's day—its occupations, stores, sicknesses, and remedies. In the same fashion she discusses Springfield—its houses and entertainment, transportation, clothes, items available in the stores, and the changes during the years Lincoln lived there. The first forty-five pages of the book deal with the same type of specific details of Lincoln's boyhood days in Kentucky and Indiana, but these details are likewise accurately descriptive of life in Illinois during the same period.

122 McKown, Robin. *Heroic Nurses.* Putnam, 1966. 320p. photos. (8 up) p.81–87, 92–96

Heroic Nurses is included in this bibliography because it contains the spirited biography of Mary Ann Bickerdyke, one of Illinois' most forceful and fascinating women. Almost nothing is available for boys and girls about this self-made nurse, whose story reveals much about the part the people of Illinois played in the Civil War. The other eleven short biographies are also worth reading. Index.

123 McNeer, May. *America's Abraham Lincoln.* Illus. by Lynd Ward. Houghton, 1957. 119p. (5–10) p.26–90

The particular strength of May McNeer's biography is that she tells Lincoln's story with extraordinary rapidity of movement, yet with no sacrifice of either clarity or important details. Lynd Ward's full-page and double-spread paintings in rich color and lovely lights and his black-and-white halftones are strong and beautiful and do as much to portray the times and character of Lincoln as the author's vivid writing. This should be one of the first Lincoln books purchased by any elementary-school library.

124 McNeer, May. *Armed with Courage.* Illus. by Lynd Ward. Abingdon, 1957. 112p. (5–8) p.55–68

The inclusion of Jane Addams among only seven of the world's many outstanding men and women of courage reveals the high regard with which this great Illinois woman is held. In a brief life story the author brings out Jane Addams's traits of character and personality, her founding of Hull House, and her other fine contributions to the improvement of the living and working conditions of laboring people.

125 McNeer, May. *Give Me Freedom.* Illus. by Lynd Ward. Abingdon, 1964. 128p. (6–9) p.54–60

Only one of the seven great workers for freedom included in this collection lived in Illinois, and then merely during the last few months of his life. But the dramatic death of Elijah P. Lovejoy, defending the Abolitionist cause and freedom of the press, took place in Alton, and for this tragedy Illinois citizens were wholly responsible. The circumstances pertaining to this unjust event are disgraceful but important in Illinois and national history.

126 McNicol, Jacqueline. *Elizabeth for Lincoln.* McKay,
1960. 119p. illus. (4–5) Fic OP

Ten-year-old Elizabeth Shires hated to sew; however, she
impressed her father's friend, whose buggy had overturned near
the Shires farm, by mending his coat exceptionally well. She
was rewarded by being allowed to accompany him from her
home near Chenoa to Springfield the day Lincoln was elected
president. When she overheard a conversation regarding danger
to Lincoln, she was sent to inform Mr. Nicolay. Later that same
day she was instrumental in thwarting a plot against Lincoln.
Real places, people, and historical events give the reader the
feeling that Elizabeth's story is basically true.

127 Martin, Patricia. *Abraham Lincoln.* Putnam (A See and
Read Biography), 1964. 64p. illus. (2–5) p.32–52

Controlled vocabulary, very short sentences, and large
print make this meager biography suitable independent reading
material for above-average second-grade readers. Little anecdotes stressing Lincoln's kindliness, his tireless efforts to educate
himself, and his deep concern over the spread of slavery will
appeal also to older reluctant readers.

128 Mason, Miriam. *Frances Willard: Girl Crusader.* Bobbs
(Childhood of Famous Americans), 1961. 200p. illus.
(3–5) p.168–92

Only the last twenty-five pages of this easy biography are
devoted to Frances Willard's adult years and to her life in
Illinois. These pages deal in limited fashion with her contributions as first dean of women at Northwestern University, as
president of the Women's Christian Temperance Union, as president of the National Council of Women, and as an active advocate of women's rights. However, even this slight coverage
will help younger children understand why her statue stands in
the Hall of Fame in Washington, D. C.

129 Meadowcroft, Enid. *Abraham Lincoln.* Illus. by Kurt
Wiese. Crowell, 1942. 191p. (5–8) p.46–127

This biography, which begins with the Lincolns' move to
Indiana and closes with Abraham Lincoln's death, is an understanding account of Lincoln, his family, and his closest asso-

ciates. The book does particularly well in presenting his stand on the slavery question and in showing his relationship with his own boys. A reasonably good idea of life in Coles County in the early 1830s, in New Salem in the 1830s, and in Springfield in the 1840s and '50s is presented. A number of important political figures are introduced, and there is a clear explanation of the state of politics in Illinois during the two decades preceding the Civil War.

130　Meadowcroft, Enid.　*By Secret Railway.*　Crowell, 1948. 275p. illus. (4–7) p.1–131, 250–72 Fic

David Morgan, living in Chicago in the 1860s, decides to leave school and get a job on the waterfront. His search for a job brings him the friendship of Jim, a young freed slave from Kentucky. When Jim loses his freedom papers, he is kidnapped by a slave catcher and taken to Missouri. David's attempt to rescue Jim leads to danger, adventure, and a long trek into Missouri. With the help of the Underground Railroad, David and Jim return to Chicago and freedom. This book will give young people an excellent idea of how the Underground Railroad functioned and a vivid picture of Chicago during the time of the Republican convention and campaign of 1860.

131　Meredith, Robert, and E. Brooks Smith, eds.　*Exploring the Great River: Early Voyagers on the Mississippi from De Soto to La Salle.*　Illus. by Leonard Fisher. Little, 1969. 151p. (7 up) p.50–67, 74–75, 82–88, 125–37

Two of these eyewitness accounts pertain to Illinois—one about the explorations of Marquette and Joliet (related by Father Marquette himself), the other about those of La Salle (related by Father Zenobius Membré). Detailed descriptions of rivers, river banks, wildlife, Indians and their ways enhance the historical events recorded. These direct presentations of their experiences by actual participants make incidents and surroundings of long ago seem very real. Maps. Index.

132　Meyer, Edith.　*Champions of the Four Freedoms.*　Little, 1966. 301p. illus. (7 up) p.28–43, 166–77

Two of the eighteen "champions of the four freedoms"

included in this book are from Illinois. One of the biographies is about Julia Lathrop who, before becoming the first chief of the Children's Bureau, had been an active resident at Hull House, a volunteer visitor for the Cook County agent's office, and a moving spirit behind the creation in Chicago of the first juvenile court in the world. She was also the driving force that started many organizations, such as the Illinois Immigrants' Protective League and the Chicago School of Civics and Philanthropy, both of which, directly or indirectly, helped improve conditions for children. The other Illinois biography is that of Elijah Lovejoy, a newspaper editor in Alton and gives vivid accounts of Lovejoy's harrowing experiences and of his murder because of his attempt to promote the cause of the freedom of the press. Index.

133 **Miers, Earl Schenck.** *Abraham Lincoln in Peace and War.*
American Heritage (American Heritage Junior Library), 1964. 153p. illus. (6–9) p.24–85
The development of Lincoln's political ideas, efforts, and successes are emphasized in this straightforward, full-length biography. Consequently the book is especially worthwhile for its presentation of political activity in Illinois and for relating that activity to the national politics of the period. These difficult matters are treated clearly and effectively enough to interest readers in junior and senior high school. Index.

134 **Miers, Earl Schenck.** *That Lincoln Boy.* World, 1968. 141p. illus. (5–8) p.98–141
An experienced writer for young people tells the story of Lincoln from his babyhood to the day he left New Salem for Springfield. An abundance of anecdotes and conversations—often humorous—show the young Lincoln as a droll, hardworking, earnest, intelligent, vital personality. A wealth of information about Illinois pioneer life and people is an important contribution of this lively biography.

135 **Miller, Helen.** *George Rogers Clark: Frontier Fighter.*
Putnam (American Pioneer Biographies), 1968. 95p. illus. (4–6) p.25–59, 74–77

Beginning with Clark at the age of nineteen, as he leaves Fort Pitt to seek land and adventure down the Ohio, this biography chronicles his conquest of Kaskaskia, Cahokia, and Vincennes, his difficulties with the Virginia government, and his unhonored, poverty-stricken last years. The fast pace of the story and the vivid presentation of the hardships, courage, and accomplishments of Clark and his men make this a very readable book. The clear account of conditions and activities in Illinois country during Revolutionary times contributes valuable historical information. Index.

136 **Mooney, Elizabeth.** *Jane Addams.* Follett (Library of American Heroes), 1968. 156p. photos. (5–8) p.7–40, 52–156

This gives a fairly detailed and substantial account of the life of Jane Addams, one of the world's greatest social workers, from her seventh year until her death. It tells of her happy childhood in Cedarville, Illinois, of her early struggle with ill health, of her passionate desire to be of service to the poor, and of her successful contributions to the improvement of the living and working conditions of Chicago's laboring classes. Vivid descriptions and sympathetic narrations re-create life in Hull House and its pathetic, filthy neighborhood. The unsentimental and yet appealing portrayal of service to others will make this biography genuinely satisfying to girls. The book has unusually attractive photographs. Index.

137 **Myers, Elisabeth.** *George Pullman: Young Sleeping Car Builder.* Bobbs (Childhood of Famous Americans), 1963. 200p. illus. (3–5) p.173–92

Since George Pullman did not come to Illinois until he was a young man, only the last few pages of this book are significant in a study of the state. However, those few pages are pertinent because they tell of the early efforts of a man who later became one of Chicago's most successful industralists, the founder of one of the earliest company-owned towns in our country, and the infamous employer, responsible for the first national railroad strike. This easy book does not go into the later unfortunate events of his career. Chronology.

138 **Myron, Robert.** *Shadow of the Hawk: Saga of the Mound Builders.* Putnam, 1964. 189p. illus. (6 up) p.78, 85–86, 94, 102, 108–15

This "saga" of the development of the ancient culture of the Mound Builders gives an excellent idea of how archeologists gather information about early peoples by piecing together the "finds" they gradually obtain from "digs." The early peoples dealt with here inhabited a vast territory north and south of the Ohio River about 2000 years ago. Because the center of this culture was in Ohio, most of the book deals with Ohio mounds. However, what has been learned from the "finds" in Ohio, particularly of the Hopewell Indians, pertained to these same Indians in Illinois. Discussions in this book of Illinois mounds and of artifacts in Illinois museums can make visits to these mounds and museums both interesting and profitable. Index.

139 **Naden, Corinne.** *The Chicago Fire, 1871: The Blaze That Nearly Destroyed a City.* Watts (Focus Book), 1969. 66p. photos. (6–9)

The vivid account of this terrible disaster includes causes of the fire, its progress, the hindrances to success in fighting it, and both immediate and far-reaching consequences. The horror of the situation is made impressive through detailed descriptions and many illustrations. Six excellent, simple maps help the reader follow the exact path of the fire. Index.

140 **Nathan, Adele, and W. C. Baker.** *Famous Railroad Stations of the World.* Random (Gateway Books), 1953. 100p. illus. (5–9) p.75–79

Along with the history of railroad stations and fascinating facts about them, the reader can gather from this book a surprising amount of information about the development of railroads. Despite the limited number of pages dealing with Illinois, the book is significant because it makes clear the importance of Chicago as a trans-shipping point for the nation. In it is a good explanation of the building of the Grand Central Station and a description of its exterior and interior. It also lists the railroads this terminal serves and those served by other Chicago terminals. Index.

141 Nathan, Adele. *Seven Brave Companions.* Illus. by Fritz Kredel. Dutton, 1953. 164p. (4–8) p.98–122, 142–52

After a brief account of the childhood and education of Marquette and of Joliet, the book tells the story of their journey down the Mississippi to the Arkansas River and their return by way of the Illinois. It brings out particularly well the fact that Marquette's purpose was to convert the Indians and Joliet's to claim the land for France. Information regarding Marquette's last days may be questioned. This book could be read by good fourth-grade readers; however, it would not insult eighth-grade readers. The lack of maps is limiting.

142 Nathan, Dorothy. *Women of Courage.* Random, 1964. 187p. illus. (6–9) p.40–73

Since there are only five women included in this collection, the full-length story of each is fairly complete. In that of Jane Addams there are not only those facts about her that would interest young people but also those that truly portray her greatness, her important contributions to the betterment of social conditions in Chicago, and the significant example she set for others who continued her efforts toward social reform and world peace. Realistic details of life of the upper middle class in a northern Illinois rural community in the mid-1800s and of the poverty-stricken in Chicago in the late 1800s fall naturally into this biography.

143 Neyhart, Louise. *Giant of the Yards.* Houghton, 1952. 218p. illus. (6–10) p.28–65, 75–140, 150–218 OP

This book is of triple value. It gives the story of Gustavus Franklin Swift from his tenth year until his death in 1903; it portrays interestingly the development of the great meat-packing industry during the last quarter of the nineteenth century; it delineates clearly improvements made through the beginning of labor organizations, housing projects, and settlement work. Among its minor contributions are glimpses of social life, outstanding Chicago people, the Columbian Exposition, and the means of transportation during the period covered.

144 Neyhart, Louise. *Henry's Lincoln.* Holiday, 1958. 50p. illus. (3–6) Fic

Henry, a farm boy living near Freeport, went alone to hear Lincoln and Douglas debate in 1858. Although Henry began the day a "Douglas man," he ended it a "Lincoln man." The incident offers little opportunity for action or for story interest; yet the author succeeds in bringing both the event and the characters to life. The important points of the debate are presented clearly enough for the understanding of a fourth grader. Details of everyday life in Illinois in the 1850s are accurate and natural. Nine full-page illustrations add to the attractiveness of the book.

145 Noble, Iris. *Clarence Darrow: Defense Attorney.* Messner, 1958. 192p. (7 up) p.25–76, 108–11, 135–50, 184–85

This thorough biography covers the same material found in Faber's *Clarence Darrow* (no. 52 on this list) but treats each aspect and each event of Darrow's life much more intensively, extensively, and understandingly. Several famous trials in which Darrow served as attorney are narrated in such realistic detail that they are as good reading as dramas. Through these narrations, not only procedures and accomplishments of this great lawyer are emphasized, but also his constant efforts to establish just opportunities for all downtrodden people. Two of the trials presented in detail pertain specifically to Illinois— the famous Pullman strike trial and the Loeb-Leopold case. The book throws considerable light upon labor conditions and the development of unions in Illinois. Index.

146 Noble, Iris. *Labor's Advocate: Eugene V. Debs.* Messner, 1966. 191p. (8 up) p.68–70, 83–84, 93–116, 121–33, 137–38, 146–47, 181

As the author tells the life story of a much-loved, much-criticized leader, she is also relating the history of labor unions in the United States. Emphasizing the capabilities, unselfishness, and tenderness of the man, the book shows, at the same time, his weaknesses and mistakes. The Illinois portions of the book give good explanations of the Haymarket Riot, the Pullman and American Railway Union strikes, the Debs conspiracy trial, and the formation of the Social Democracy Party, and later of the Industrial Workers of the World (IWW). George Pullman, Peter Altgeld, and Clarence Darrow, well-known Illinois citizens, are accorded the same fair treatment given Debs. Index.

147 **Nolan, Jeannette.** *Abraham Lincoln.* Illus. by Lee Ames. Messner, 1953. 182p. (6 up) p.45–121

One of the most readable biographies of Lincoln written for young people, this covers his life from his seventh year until his death. The book gives a just and sympathetic portrayal of the man and reveals with clarity and simplicity the state and national problems with which he was vitally concerned. At the head of each chapter is a black-and-white drawing which shows Lincoln as he probably looked during the time depicted in the chapter. These successive pictures make a good study of the development of his character. Index.

148 **Nolan, Jeannette.** *The Gay Poet: The Story of Eugene Field.* Messner, 1940. 260p. illus. (7 up) p.114–37, 209–54

This story of Eugene Field's life begins when Field was six and ends with his death in 1895. It is more alive than most biographies of authors because it includes many pranks of his boyhood and youth and examples of the humor of his later years. A good picture of Knox College during the years 1869 and 1871 is found in the account of Field's freshman and sophomore years there. The last fifty pages portray Field as a columnist on the *Chicago Daily News* and as an almost ideal husband and father. In these same pages many contemporary important business and newspaper men with whom Field associated are briefly introduced.

149 **Nolan, Jeannette.** *George Rogers Clark: Soldier and Hero.* Illus. by Lee Ames. Messner, 1954. 190p. (6 up) p.86–125, 144–46

The story of Clark is told here from the time he left his father's comfortable Virginia home until his last years, spent in his sister's home in Kentucky. Better than most books, this one makes clear his realization that taking the Western forts was necessary to prevent Britain and her Indian allies from attacking the colonies in the West and thus getting the upper hand in the Revolution. This realization furnished Clark with the drive which resulted in his capture of Forts Kaskaskia and Vincennes and his repeated success in Indian warfare. The faithful account of these hard-won successes makes the book very readable. Index.

150 Nolan, Jeannette. *La Salle and the Grand Enterprise.* Messner, 1951. 178p. (6–9) p.81–94, 99–104, 112–14

This book is better written and somewhat more difficult than the Graham and the Syme biographies of La Salle (nos. 70 and 185 respectively on this list). Through her use of conversation the author delineates characters sharply and realistically. The lure of the Mississippi for La Salle, and the devotion of Saget, Nika, and Tonti to him, permeate the action. For the sake of information on Illinois it is regrettable that La Salle's first trip down the Illinois River is omitted. A map of La Salle's other journeys contributes to the usefulness of the book. Index.

151 Nolan, Jeannette. *The Little Giant: Stephen A. Douglas.* Messner, 1964. 191p. (6–9) p.46–183

The author has included in this just portrayal enough of the personal and exciting to make a very readable book for young people. The portion devoted to Douglas in Illinois stresses his relationship with Lincoln and thereby reveals the events of one of the most significant periods in the state's history. There is information about the life of the times and about people and places in Illinois. Appendixes contain excerpts from the Lincoln-Douglas debates. Index.

152 Nolan, Jeannette. *The Story of Ulysses S. Grant.* Illus. by Lynd Ward. Grosset (Signature Books), 1952. 180p. (4–7) p.116–36

This story of Grant's life covers the years of his childhood through his inauguration as president of the United States. The language is oversimplified, but humorous, daring, and fast-moving events make the book appealing to boys and girls in the intermediate grades and to retarded older readers. Not many pages are devoted to Illinois, but enough to show why the state includes Grant as one of her famous sons.

153 Nolan, Jeannette. *The Victory Drum.* Illus. by Lorence F. Bjorklund. Messner, 1953. 152p. (4–7) p.3–87 Fic OP

This somewhat fictionalized account of the famous march of George Rogers Clark from Kaskaskia to Vincennes centers around a twelve-year-old drummer boy. Plenty of action and the fine relationship between the boy and his comrades make the story as entertaining as fiction. Since three-fourths of the book is set in Illinois and most of the details are factual, there is good Illinois information. (Can be obtained in paperback— Washington Square, Archway 29005)

154 North, Sterling. *Abe Lincoln: Log Cabin to White House.* Illus. by Lee Ames. Random (Landmark Books), 1956. 178p. (5 up) p.65–172

Of the many biographies of Abraham Lincoln written for boys and girls, this one is better than average because it depends upon the attractiveness of his personality, the vigor and genuineness of his actions, and the force of his own words to hold the interest of the reader rather than upon fictionalized activities and conversation. Moreover, it is well written. It is especially good for use in an Illinois study, for it emphasizes not only Lincoln but other Midwest characters. Index.

155 Orrmont, Arthur. *Master Detective: Allan Pinkerton.* Messner, 1965. 191p. (7–12) p.31–58, 125–33, 177–82

Beginning in Glasgow when Pinkerton was twelve, this narrative biography tells of his life as a youth in Scotland, as a cooper in Dundee, Illinois, and as a successful detective at the head of the famous Pinkerton Agency in Chicago. Included are many incidents of his helping Negroes escape by the Underground Railroad. Most attractive to boys and girls are the stories of famous cases handled by the master sleuth and his men, such as their overcoming the notorious Reno Gang, their breaking up the tough Molly Maguires, their uncovering a plot to assassinate Lincoln. Boys and girls in the Onarga, Illinois, region will be particularly interested in the description of Pinkerton's country home there. Index.

156 Peithmann, Irvin. *Indians of Southern Illinois.* Charles C. Thomas, 1964. 125p. photos. (7 up)
After giving an account of the daily life and customs of the Indians of Southern Illinois through four prehistoric cultures —Archaic, Woodland, Hopewellian, and Mississippi—the author discusses the languages, transportation, medicine, mythology, religion, traditions, legends, and magic of historic Indian cultures before the white man. The last section of the book deals with the relationship between the Indians and the first white men who came to this region and the eventual subjugation of the Indians. The approach is so mature and the material so detailed that no boy or girl is likely to read the whole book, but pertinent portions can be profitably used for specific assignments. Index.

157 Perl, Lila. *Red-Flannel Hash and Shoo-fly Pie: American Regional Foods and Festivals.* World, 1965. 288p. (7 up) p.144–71, 180–83
"This book tells the story of what Americans eat, and why. To tell this story, it reaches back four hundred years into the history of the United States and ranges the breadth of that land from Maine to Hawaii." This first paragraph of the introduction expresses accurately what the book accomplishes. Treating eight regions separately, it describes fascinatingly the eating habits and food of each and gives two or three typical recipes. History, geography, tradition, and culinary customs are logically interwoven. The pages indicated above deal with various parts of the Midwest, but the material included is in general applicable to Illinois. Index.

158 Peterson, Harold. *Forts in America.* Scribner, 1964. 61p. illus. (5 up) p.42–44
The introduction states that the book "traces the major developments in the design and construction of permanent forts in the United States." This is successfully accomplished through clear descriptions and excellent drawings and diagrams of more

than a dozen famous forts, discussed chronologically according to the time of their building. Among the best known are Jamestown, Ticonderoga, McHenry, Dearborn, Laramie, Sumter. Only Fort Dearborn belongs to Illinois, and its treatment in this book is brief, but it would be difficult to find a more graphic description and better illustration of its construction. Index.

159 **Peterson, Helen.** *Jane Addams: Pioneer of Hull House.* Garrard (A Discovery Book), 1965. 80p. (2–4)
This biography of Jane Addams from early childhood until death, briefly gives the successive events in her life and particularly emphasizes her successful efforts to improve living and working conditions of the poor. Because it was written for reluctant readers (reading level is third grade and interest level third up), the style is choppy and tiresome. However, properly used it will serve a purpose.

160 **Place, Marian.** *John Wesley Powell: Canyon's Conqueror.* Houghton (Piper Books), 1963. 191p. illus. (5–7) p.74–76, 80–92, 101–5, 123, 137, 181
A biography of John Wesley Powell can contribute only a small amount to information on Illinois. Yet two Illinois colleges, Illinois Wesleyan and Illinois State University, point with pride to the fact that he was at one time in their science departments. Since the science program at Wesleyan was closely coordinated with that of the Illinois State Natural History Society, Powell became active in that organization. Thus it was through the sponsorship and partial aid of the Illinois State Natural History Society that Powell made his famous explorations in the Colorado River Valley. This story makes evident the contribution of Illinois to Powell's success. Maps.

161 **Pliss, Louise.** *The Strange Journey of Kippy Brooks.* Reilly, 1965. 121p. illus. (3–5) p.33–39, 48–114 Fic OP
Kippy, too small to play with the big boys and too big to play with the small boys, climbs into a box car and is accidentally carried from a New York village to Chicago. Alone, he wanders from place to place in the city until he falls into Lake Michigan, is rescued by a sailor, and retrieved by his parents.

His day of wandering enables the author to impress a country child with the bewildering, impersonal hustle and bustle of Chicago and to call his attention to a few Chicago places.

162 Potter, Marian. *Copperfield Summer.* Follett, 1967. 160p. illus. (5–7)

In spite of the too-frequently-used situation of children having to be sent to a relative because of their mother's illness, this recounting of the experiences of Ann and Ted on Aunt Til's farm in southern Illinois has value. Their adventures in keeping up with the lively children of shiftless neighbors, coping with a sick vagabond in an empty church, and living through the devastation of a cyclone make interesting reading. The background against which these adventures are presented gives a vivid picture of everyday rural life in Little Egypt in 1925.

163 Randall, Ruth. *I Mary, A Biography of the Girl Who Married Lincoln.* Little, 1959. 242p. illus. (7 up) p.36–92, 101–43, 210–33

No book of fiction could be more appealing to a romantic teen-age girl than this extremely sympathetic and idealistic portrayal of Lincoln's impulsive, tragic wife. The personal characteristics of those close to her and the important events in their lives as well as many details of the way of upper-class life in Springfield in the 1840s and '50s are woven naturally into this biography. It would be difficult to find anywhere in literature for young people so convincing a debunking of the Ann Rutledge legend. Index.

164 Randall, Ruth. *Lincoln's Animal Friends.* Little, 1958. 152p. illus. (5–8) p.3–11, 54–114

Obviously, the purpose of this book is to emphasize Lincoln's innate love for animals. It relates many incidents which tell about Lincoln and pets, farm animals, and homeless, unfortunate creatures. These incidents make interesting reading for children, giving them a feeling of intimacy with the Lincoln family and impressing them with Lincoln's gentle nature and his thorough enjoyment of the simplest things in life. The author disposes of the Ann Rutledge romance with certainty as a legend. She portrays Mary Lincoln as a likeable, attractive person, with almost no hint that she was ever otherwise. There are touches of sentimentality and didacticism. A helpful time schedule of events in Lincoln's life is found at the end of the book.

165 **Rátz, Margaret.** *Exploring Chicago.* Follett, 1965. 128p. illus. (4–6) OP

Through the devices of imaginary trips and school lessons, the author gives a clear overview of the Chicago area and important information regarding its transportation, educational opportunities, government, history, famous people, museums, parks, buildings, fairs, shopping areas, homes, landmarks. Fifteen drawings and diagrams, nine maps, and over one hundred photographs, together with other helpful features such as questions and lists of related books, make this a useful textbook and good general reading. Index.

166 **Rauch, Mabel.** *The Little Hellion.* Duell, 1960. (Dist. by Meredith) 180p. (6–9) Fic OP

Portrayal of a distinctive way of life characteristic of southern Illinois at the turn of the century makes this a useful book. Though the "Little Hellion," Sally, is only nine at the beginning of the story, her recounting of exciting episodes which touch Judge Chalfont's family in "Egypt" will keep upper-graders reading to the end. With her they will bring the romance between two lovers from feuding families to a happy ending and will savor the long-delayed reunion of a Confederate veteran and his Northern sweetheart. They will share the mixed emotions of the gypsy, Zilka, who loves her foster parents but cannot resist the call of the music of her own people. Horse lovers and racing fans have a satisfying surprise ending as they view, with the author, the race between the Judge's "biggest horse in Egypt" and the Doc's Little Billy.

167 **Rauch, Mabel.** *Vinnie and the Flag-Tree: A Novel of the Civil War in Southern Illinois—America's Egypt.* Duell, 1959. 149p. (8–10) Fic OP

Sixteen-year-old Vinnie volunteers to leave her rural home near Carbondale to become a nurse in the improvised Union Army hospital in Cairo. After the soldiers are moved farther south, she helps pass the long years of waiting for the return of her soldier-husband by taking every possible opportunity to aid in the war effort. Her chief contribution is the dangerous climb she makes to lower the flag that warns the neighborhood of the presence of enemy spies. The story, based on historical fact, is good, but the worth of the book is its poignant portrayal of the heartbreaking division of loyalties among neighbors, friends, and members of a family living in "Little Egypt." Young readers will receive a pleasant impression of General and Mrs. Logan and will obtain a good explanation of the Golden Circle, an organization of Northerners in sympathy with the South. In addition, the book gives an account of the first Memorial Day.

168 Ray, Bert. *We Live in the City.* Childrens Press (Reading Laboratory Book), 1963. unpaged. illus. (1–2)

This quick look at Chicago describes in very easy language such significant aspects of the city as the zoo, airport, museum, art fair, skyscrapers, Chinatown. Colorful, poster-style illustrations on every page and a good, simple map add interest and clarity.

169 Raymond, Charles. *The Trouble with Gus.* Follett, 1968. 256p. illus. (6–9) Fic

A crowded north-side Chicago area, inhabited by "hillbillies," American Indians, Negroes, and a variety of Europeans, is the setting for the story of the girl, Gus, who longs to move to an attractive suburb as her best friend has done. The problems arising from the mixture of peoples and the poverty of the neighborhood, and from her home with a jobless father, are real, present-day problems of an inner-city section of Chicago. The help given to Gus and her schoolmates by the social workers in a new settlement house is typical of the contributions made at such institutions to the welfare of young people in underprivileged communities. The account of a short auto trip north on the Outer Drive taken by Gus and her parents gives excellent descriptions of scenes along the shore of Lake Michigan.

170   Raymond, Charles. *Up from Appalachia.* Follett, 1966. 191p. (6–10) Fic

Nine-year-old Lathe Cantrell moves with his family from a poverty-stricken Kentucky area to a poverty-stricken Chicago area. Added to the seeming hopelessness of getting jobs are the heartbreak of being ostracized because they are "hillbillies" and the longing for the out-of-doors. Thanks to determined Gramma, the dump heap next door is turned into a garden and playground, the young toughs into a friendly club, and the neighbors of all ages into an harmonious folk-music group. The Cantrells' successful efforts to get jobs and to adjust to city life make it possible for the author to present realistic Chicago scenes and conditions; however, the characters and the outcome of their actions are often too good to be true.

171   Redway, Maurine, and Dorothy Bracken. *Marks of Lincoln on Our Land.* Hastings, 1957. 117p. photos. (6 up) p.39–83

This biography of Lincoln is unique in its approach in that it outlines the story of his life through the monuments and shrines raised in his honor. It is in no sense a juvenile book, yet it is of value in an elementary library because of the thirty-nine excellent photographs (most of them full page) of statues and memorials and of places intimately connected with Lincoln. Of these, twenty are located in Illinois. These photographs should inspire Illinois boys and girls and their parents to make visits to Lincoln shrines. To increase the worth and enjoyment of these visits, parents and children should read the text together.

172   Roesch, Roberta. *World's Fairs: Yesterday, Today, Tomorrow.* Day, 1964. 96p. (5–9) p.29–34, 49–55

Two of the thirteen world's fairs discussed here were held in Chicago—the World's Columbian Exposition in 1893 and the Century of Progress in 1933–34. The discussions point up briefly the main attractions of each. For the Columbian Exposition the emphasis is upon the Ferris wheel and the exhibits that portrayed the development of industry and invention. Since the Century of Progress had a double purpose—to honor a hundred years of progress in science and industry and to celebrate Chicago's hundredth birthday—there are chiefly descriptions of the demonstrations that presented advancements in science and invention and of exhibits that represented periods in America's past. In spite of its brevity the book does well in giving a realization of the educational values of fairs and the feeling of their significance. Index.

173 Rosenheim, Lucile. *Kathie: The New Teacher.* Messner, 1949. 195p. (6–10) Fic
The author has effectively presented the school and social problems of an inexperienced teacher in a town small enough for the schoolteacher's life to be everybody's concern. The problems are those of most young teachers in a small town; the specific background details are those of an Illinois community on Lake Michigan north of Chicago in the middle of the twentieth century.

174 Sandburg, Carl. *Prairie-Town Boy.* Harcourt, 1955. 179p. illus. (7 up)
This is more than an informal, detailed autobiographical account of the first twenty years of Sandburg's life. It is a good general picture of Galesburg in the late 1800s and an introduction to a number of Galesburg citizens who were prominent in state and national affairs at that time. It is particularly valuable in bringing out the place and characteristics of Swedish immigrants in northern Illinois and the details of the way of life of the hard-working, ambitious, intelligent, Midwestern town families of lower economic status in the half-century after the Civil War.

175 Sattley, Helen. *Annie.* Dodd, 1961. 183p. illus. (6–9) Fic OP
Thirteen-year-old Annie, her three brothers, three sisters, and their mother join their father in Chicago just after the great fire. As the story describes the experiences of this English family's becoming adjusted to their new home, it also tells of the rapid and fine rebuilding of the city. English, German, and Scotch songs, Indian tales and American verse, an American-Irish Hallowe'en, an American Thanksgiving, an English Christ-

mas, an American sleigh ride, and an English Maypole dance reveal the varied background of a developing American culture. Although the bit of plot is solved by unlikely coincidence, factual details are accurate and individual incidents convincing.

176 Selvin, David. *Champions of Labor.* Abelard, 1967. 256p. photos. (8 up) p.42–44, 78–89, 97–98, 141–47

These accounts of thirteen outstanding leaders give a clear idea of the development of labor unions in the United States. Significant incidents occurring in Illinois appear in several. The Haymarket riot, the Pullman strike, the organizing in Chicago of the Industrial Workers of the World and the Chicago Hart, Schaffner and Marx strike are recounted in the biographies of Powderly, Debs, Haywood, and Hillman respectively. A glossary of "terms frequently used in trade union and industrial relations language" and an appendix of short sketches of the lives of outstanding labor leaders will prove useful.

177 Selvin, David. *Eugene Debs: Rebel, Labor Leader, Prophet.* Lothrop, 1966. 192p. photos. (8 up) p.69–149

This is a full-length, factual biography of Eugene Debs, who won international fame as active labor leader, Socialist candidate for the presidency, and advocate of prison reform. As founder of the American Railway Union, he was deeply involved in the Pullman strike. When finally the case was brought to court, he was accused of conspiracy to interfere with interstate commerce. The book follows in some detail the development of labor unions, gives causes, progress, and outcome of the great Chicago-centered Pullman strike, and presents a number of prominent Illinois men—George Pullman, Governor Altgeld, and Clarence Darrow. Index.

178 Severn, Bill. *Adlai Stevenson: Citizen of the World.* McKay, 1966. 184p. illus. (8 up) p.1–18, 21–32, 52–55, 59–71, 87–109, 113–32, 162, 174–75

In addition to presenting the chronological events in the life of a great man, this biography makes the reader aware of Stevenson's political accomplishments and his constant striving towards the ideals of peace and brotherhood. His fine relationship with his sons and his love for his Libertyville home are particularly emphasized. The book shows clearly how likeable, witty, and genuine he was. Quotations from his speeches and writings illustrate his cleverness in thinking and in handling words. Details of Bloomington, Springfield, and Chicago add good Illinois background material. Index.

179 Silverberg, Robert. *Bridges.* Macrae, 1966. 189p. photos. (6–9) p.67–78

After making clear the extreme need for a bridge across the Mississippi from St. Louis to Illinois, the text gives facts to show the tremendous hazards which would be involved in building such a bridge. Then follows a brief account of the accomplishments of James Eads, the man who assumed the responsibility of carrying out the undertaking. The step-by-step explanation of the methods of procedure employed between the start of construction in 1867 and the successful completion of the bridge in 1874 includes discussions of materials and machinery used and of the many difficulties encountered. Index.

180 Simon, Charlie May. *Lays of the New Land.* Dutton, 1943. 254p. illus. (7 up) Scattered pages

Pages 145 to 157 give some information about Edgar Lee Masters as a boy in Petersburg and later in Lewistown. There is also a bit about him in Chicago after he became a lawyer. This information is well selected for older boys and girls and interestingly presented. A few of Masters's poems, those about Illinois, are also included. Almost none of the brief biography of Vachel Lindsay in this book (pages 199–209) has to do with his life in Illinois. Pages 187 to 198 give a good account of Carl Sandburg's life, much of which was spent in Illinois.

181 Smith, Eunice. [The Jennifer Books] Bobbs. ca. 250 pages each. illus. Fic

181a *The Jennifer Wish,* 1949. (4–6)
181b *The Jennifer Gift,* 1950. (4–6)
181c *The Jennifer Prize,* 1951. (4–6)
181d *Jennifer Is Eleven,* 1952. (5–6)

181e *Jennifer Dances*, 1954. (5–7)

181f *High Heels for Jennifer*, 1964. (6–8)

Each of the first four [Jennifer] books presents several months in the lives of the Hills, a typical middle-class family living on an Illinois farm near Aurora in the first quarter of this century. The fifth gives an account of the winter Jennifer lived in her aunt's beautiful home on Rush Street in Chicago. In the sixth, Jennifer is back home, concerned with horses, boys, and other early-teen-age interests. Geographic details are so accurate that one familiar with the Aurora area and Chicago's Near North Side can easily recognize specific places. These stories have value as reading material that portrays vividly the various phases of farm and city life in the first two decades of the 1900s. Transportation, homes, food, clothing, pets, toys, play, work, school, reading, holidays are true to time and place. The writing and plots are far from outstanding, but the characters are natural and wholesome and the incidents realistic, often humorous. Each book is complete in itself.

182 **Smith, Fredrika.** *Wilderness Adventure.* Rand-McNally, 1958. 176p. illus. (5–8) p.(9–86), 150–76 Fic OP

Through the story of the fine friendship of a Potawatomi boy and the son of a settler, details concerning village life on the banks of the Chicago River in 1811 and exciting incidents leading to the Fort Dearborn massacre of 1812 are vividly portrayed. There is also a glimpse of the white man's settlement on Lake Peoria. Though escape from extreme danger is too frequently recurrent, the book on the whole is reasonably plausible.

183 **Smucker, Barbara.** *Wigwam in the City.* Dutton, 1966. 154p. illus. (4–7) p. 61–154 Fic

Susan Bearskin and her parents, Chippewa Indians, are reluctant to leave their Wisconsin reservation in spite of its lack of even the necessities of life. Although Chicago gives them work and consequently good food, clothing, and shelter, adjustment to so different a way of life is difficult. The story is somber but interesting in detail and incident. It is particularly valuable for its realistic portrayal of the unfortunate conditions of contemporary Indians on reservations and in urban relocations. It also provides boys and girls with an awareness of the problems that confront Indians who move to the cities.

184 **Stanek, Muriel.** *You and Chicago.* Benefic (Basic Social Studies Series), 1964. 191p. illus. (4–6) p.4–139, 180–91

Well organized and clear, this semi-textbook gives surprisingly thorough coverage of such matters as history, people, transportation, communications, trade, government, education, recreation, places. In addition to the information on Chicago, the book gives a quick survey of the cities and parks of Illinois and of great cities elsewhere in the world. Excellent maps and many pictures add interest and usefulness.

185 **Syme, Ronald.** *La Salle of the Mississippi.* Illus. by William Stobbs. Morrow, 1953. 184p. (6–9) p.61–109, 122–29

La Salle's unrelenting determination to win the Mississippi Valley for France and his skill in gaining the friendship of the Indians are particularly well brought out in this biography filled with adventure and action. The accounts of the exploration of the Illinois River and the portrayal of the Illinois Indians make the book valuable in the study of Illinois. Actual quotes from source material give the reader a feeling of authenticity. Strong black-and-white pictures and a good end-paper map of La Salle's America contribute to the usefulness of the book.

186 **Taylor, Florance.** *Jim Long-Knife.* Whitman, 1959. 174p. illus. (5–8) p.74–149 Fic

Jim Hudson, a fourteen-year-old Kentucky lad, is captured by the Potawatomi Indians, who call him Jim Long-Knife. Jim escapes and joins the forces of George Rogers Clark before he captures the fort at Kaskaskia. From the account of the following seven months we learn of the life of the French habitants at Kaskaskia, of the importance of the Church in the colony, and of Clark's relationship with the Illinois Indians. The book ends with the desperate 240-mile march of Clark's troops through the "freezing water and half-frozen mud" of lower Illinois, and their successful capture of Fort Sackville at Vincennes.

187 **Vance, Marguerite.** *The Lamp Lighters: Women in the Hall of Fame.* Dutton, 1960. 254p. illus. (8–12) p.208–20

The Lamp Lighters is a collection of biographies of the eight women who are included in the Hall of Fame for Great Americans. Frances E. Willard came from Wisconsin to Northwestern Female College in Evanston at the age of twenty and remained in that neighborhood most of her life. As recording secretary of the American Methodist Ladies Centenary Association, dean of women at Northwestern University, vice-president of the Association for the Advancement of Women, and corresponding secretary and later president of the Women's Christian Temperance Union, she contributed widely to the political, cultural, and intellectual advancement of women in this country. The twenty-five pages devoted to her give not only a straightforward, honest account of her life from birth to death, but also a good presentation of the outstanding historical events of her day.

188 **Veglahn, Nancy.** *Peter Cartwright: Pioneer Circuit Rider.* Scribner, 1968. 192p. (8 up) p.106–56, 167–88

The story of a minister's life may not seem very promising reading for young people, but this biography has zest. Peter Cartwright, an itinerant Methodist preacher, came from Kentucky to Illinois in 1824 with his wife and children. His sense of humor, hearty friendliness, robust manner, boisterous eloquence, physical strength, and complete fearlessness made him a hero among the rough frontiersmen and will make him an attractive character to modern boys and girls. Not only as the most famous pioneer minister of his day but also as a state legislator and Lincoln's opponent in a race for Congress is Peter Cartwright a part of Illinois history. Index.

189 **Wagoner, Jean.** *Jane Addams: Little Lame Girl.* Bobbs (Childhood of Famous Americans), 1944. 192p. illus. (3–5)

This simple biography begins with Jane Addams at the age of five and follows her through her childhood in the little town of Cedarville, Illinois. Only a few pages are devoted to her life at Rockford College and abroad, and only a few to the founding of Hull House. The author has done well in bringing out those characteristics in the child which developed into the peculiar greatness of the woman, Jane Addams. Several major occupations are well represented in this good picture of life in a northern Illinois town in the 1860s and 1870s. There are also glimpses of Freeport.

190 Ward, Martha. *Adlai Stevenson: Young Ambassador.* Bobbs (Childhood of Famous Americans), 1967. 200p. illus. (3–5) p.32–75, 117–43, 159–60, 172–86

The author of this easy biography depends upon anecdotes to present the young Stevenson as a natural, alert, intelligent boy. Since his family before him as well as Stevenson himself were in both state and national politics, the book includes a number of facts about outstanding Illinois citizens and visitors and relates interesting bits. of Illinois history. Especially vivid are the scenes and details of daily life of the Bloomington-Normal area. The portion devoted to the adult life of Stevenson may help make young readers aware of his contributions to our state government and to world peace.

191 Weaver, John. *Tad Lincoln: Mischief-Maker in the White House.* Dodd, 1963. 145p. illus. (6–10) p.1–35

Weaver's biography of Lincoln's youngest son covers the years between Tad's birth and Lincoln's death. The emphasis throughout is upon the comfort and cheer the small boy brings his father in his saddest and most anxious years. Only the first thirty-five pages deal with Illinois, but those pages give a vivid picture of the everyday life of the Lincoln family in their comfortable, modest home on Eighth Street in Springfield, and a genuine realization of the unusual closeness of Lincoln and his boys. The portrayal of the fine father-son relationship and the lively recounting of Tad's pranks make fascinating reading for boys and girls. Index.

192 Wernecke, Herbert. *Tales of Christmas from Near and Far.* Westminster, 1963. 232p. (5–7) p.126–34 Fic

Clara Judson's *A Bohemian Christmas in Chicago* is included among these 33 stories from 15 different countries. In this lively account of the efforts of a wholesome Bohemian family to fit its own beloved ways of celebrating Christmas into those of a new country may be found an excellent description of downtown Chicago at Christmastime in the late 1800s. The highlight of the family's trip to the Loop is the father's explanation of a model of the coming Columbian Exposition, in which he emphasizes with pride the bringing of Bohemian glassblowers to the Fair to demonstrate their country's famous art.

193 Werstein, Irving. *Labor's Defiant Lady: The Story of Mother Jones.* Crowell, 1969. 146p. (7 up) p.20, 26–33, 45–57, 102–4, 135–36

An interesting view of labor unions in the United States is presented in this very readable biography of Mary Harris Jones. In any part of the country where trouble arose among the workers—mechanics, coal or metal miners, railroad or textile workers—"Mother Jones" could be found in the thick of the fray, rallying laborers to take a stand for their rights. Her indomitable courage in facing management, her lifelong devotion to a cause, and her absolute fearlessness in the midst of real danger make her story intense and exciting. Index.

194 Whitney, Phyllis. *A Long Time Coming.* McKay, 1954. 261p. (6–10) Fic

This teen-age novel is more than an interesting account of how Christie Allard comes to know her father after nine years of complete separation from him. It is also a vivid portrayal of the deplorable living and working conditions of the migrant workers in midwestern cornfields and canneries, and a poignant analysis of the determination of the inhabitants of a cannery town to keep these outsiders wholly apart from all town activities. It includes, too, suggestions for improving conditions even in the face of this unfortunate animosity.

195 Whitney, Phyllis. *Willow Hill.* McKay, 1947. 243p. (7–10) Fic

Val Coleman and her father, Nick, the high school coach in a town near Chicago, accept and like the Negroes who move into a housing project. When Negro teen-agers enter the high school and Nick chooses a Negro boy for the basketball team, there is trouble. This is an above-average story that tells how the students worked out a problem typical not only of Chicago's suburbs but of almost any large city suburb in our country.

196 Wibberley, Leonard. *Wes Powell: Conqueror of the Grand Canyon.* Farrar, 1958. 216p. (7 up) p.25–28, 41–45 OP

This book, like the biography of Powell by Marian Place (no. 160 on this list), contributes little information on Illinois but is included for the same reasons. It would undoubtedly be wise to purchase only one of these books for the average school library. Wibberley's is somewhat easier to read and more interestingly told. His account of Powell's expeditions in the Green and Colorado River valleys reads like a fiction adventure story. Maps, other than those on the end sheets, would add to the usefulness of the book. Index.

197 Wise, Winifred. *Jane Addams of Hull House.* Harcourt, 1935. 255p. photos. (7–10) p.3–95, 127–247

This straightforward story of the life of Jane Addams from infancy into the 1930s begins with her parents, Sarah and John Addams, who came to Cedarville, Illinois, in 1844 as a bride and groom. Many interesting facts about life in a small town in northern Illinois in the last half of the nineteenth century, about Rockford Seminary in the late 1870s and early '80s, and about the founding and first years of Hull House are included. Jane Addams' many interests introduce young readers to Chicago's early labor, immigrant, and social service problems. (Advanced readers in the eighth and ninth grades could get additional material about Jane Addams and her work at Hull House from her autobiographical *Twenty Years at Hull House*.)

198 Young, Ben T. *Rock River Ranger.* Abelard, 1953. 157p. (6–9) p.11–139 Fic OP

Both historical fiction and adventure story, this book, based upon true events in the Black Hawk War, makes several worthwhile contributions to knowledge of that period. It gives the viewpoint of white settlers actually living on Rock Island, points up the place of the Rock River Rangers in the war, and brings out exceptionally well the little details of everyday home and village life. No juvenile book has so clear a map of the Rock Island-Saukenuk environs. The style has the flavor of Midwest pioneer language with its plain phrases and frequent homely, apt comparisons.

199 **Zehnpfennig, Gladys.** *Carl Sandburg: Poet and Patriot.* Denison (315 Fifth Ave., S., Minneapolis, Minn. 55415), 1963. 265p. (8 up) p.17–152, 227–30 OP

This is an interesting biography for serious readers above the seventh grade. Pages 17 to 76 present Sandburg's first twenty years as well as details of everyday life in Galesburg in the last quarter of the nineteenth century. Pages 227 to 230 describe Sandburg's birthplace as it is restored today for visitors.

200 **Ziegler, Elsie.** *Light a Little Lamp.* Day (Daughters of Valor), 1961. 191p. (7–9) Fic OP

Nearly a third of this so-called biography of Mary Mc-Dowell is a graphic description of the Chicago fire. This event gave Miss McDowell, a famous Chicago social worker, an opportunity for dramatic service to the refugees, many of whom were poor immigrants, badly housed and overcrowded, who had been imported to furnish cheap labor for the stockyards in the 1870s. Though there is only a brief treatment of Miss McDowell's accomplishments, the story makes clear that her interest in the immigrants developed into a lifelong successful crusade to better their working and living conditions. The contrast of these conditions with those of the wealthy presents the need for labor laws and reform and shows the reason for the rapid growth of labor unions. The space devoted to important events in Mary McDowell's life is poorly proportioned and the writing is uneven, but the material is of value.

Appendixes

Suggested References

Adams, James and William Keller, (comps.) *Illinois Place Names.* (Occasional Publications no. 54) Springfield: Illinois State Historical Society, n.d. (Springfield 62706)

Allen, John. *It Happened in Southern Illinois.* Carbondale: Southern Illinois Univ. Pr., 1968.

Arnold, Pauline and Percival White. *How We Named Our States.* New York: Criterion, 1965.

Atlas of the State of Illinois. Rockford: Rockford Map Publishers, 1965. (4525 Forestview Ave., Rockford 61108)

Earle, Olive. *State Birds and Flowers.* New York: Morrow, 1951.

Earle, Olive. *State Trees.* New York: Morrow, 1964.

Federal Writers Project. *Illinois Guide.* rev. ed. New York: Hastings, 1968.

Graham, Jory. *Chicago: An Extraordinary Guide.* Chicago: Rand-McNally, 1968.

Illinois League of Women Voters. *Illinois Voters Handbook* (Biennial). Chicago: The League (67 E. Madison St., Chicago 60602)

Koeper, Frederick. *Illinois Architecture from Territorial Times to the Present: A Selective Guide.* Chicago: The Univ. of Chicago Pr., 1968. Paper.

Mohlenbrock, Robert. *The Illustrated Flora of Illinois: Ferns.* Carbondale: Southern Illinois Univ. Pr., 1967.

119

Siegel, Arthur. *Chicago's Famous Buildings.* Chicago: The Univ. of Chicago Pr., 1965.

Vogel, Virgil. *Indian Place Names in Illinois.* Springfield: Illinois State Historical Society, 1963. (Springfield 62706)

Free and Inexpensive Materials

Abraham Lincoln Chronology. James Hickey. Illinois State Historical Library, Springfield 62706

Calendar of Events. (annual) Illinois Information Service, 406 State Capitol, Springfield 62706

A Chronology of Illinois History, 1673–1962. Margaret Flint, comp. Illinois State Historical Library, Springfield 62706

Counties of Illinois. Their Origin and Evolution. rev. ed. Off. of the Secretary of State, Springfield 62706

Fourteen Illinois Trips. Div. of Tourism, Dept. of Business and Economic Development, 222 S. College Ave., Springfield 62704

Government in Illinois: State, County, Local. rev. ed. Off. of the Secretary of State, Springfield 62706

The Great Seal and Other Official State Symbols. Off. of the Secretary of State, Springfield 62706

Heirloom Cook Book. Northern Illinois Gas Co., Aurora 60504

Illinois Blue Book. (biennial) Off. of the Secretary of State, Springfield 62706

Illinois: Land of Lincoln—Inland Empire. Illinois Information Service, 406 State Capitol, Springfield 62706

Illinois Wild Flowers. John Voss and Virginia Eifert. (Popular Science Series) Illinois State Museum, Springfield 62706

Invitation To Birds. Virginia Eifert. (Story of Illinois Series) Illinois State Museum, Springfield 62706

100 Magnificent Museums in Illinois. Illinois Bell Telephone Co. (Box M, Rm. 1801, 208 W. Washington St., Chicago 60606) or from Illinois Dept. of Conservation, 113 State Office Bldg., Springfield 62706

Pond Fish and Fishing in Illinois. A. C. Lopinot. (Fishery Bulletin no.5) Illinois Dept. of Conservation, 113 State Office Bldg., Springfield 62706

Rules of the Road. Paul Powell, comp. Off. of the Secretary of State, Springfield 62706

Sanitary Requirements for Swimming Pools. Div. of Sanitary Engineering, Illinois Dept. of Public Health, Springfield 62706

The Settlement of Illinois, 1700–1850. Victor Hicken. (Studies in Illinois History) Western Illinois Univ., Macomb, or Office of the Supt. of Public Instruction, 316 S. 2d St., Springfield 62706

Stories of Historic Illinois. Joyce Thompson (ed.). Illinois Power Co., 500 S. 27th St., Decatur, Ill. 62525

The Trembling Land: Illinois in the Age of Exploration. William Burton. (Studies in Illinois History) Western Illinois Univ., Macomb, or Office of the Supt. of Public Instruction, 316 S. 2d St., Springfield 62706

Visit . . . See Historic and Scenic Illinois. (Packet of folders) Div. of Parks, Dept. of Conservation, 113 State Office Bldg., Springfield 62706

Water Resources of Illinois. Shirley Bartell. State Water Survey Div., Dept. of Registration and Education, Box 232, Urbana 61801

Books about Athletes and Sports

The books in this list, each of which has direct connection with Illinois, contribute very little information about the state. Yet such books may serve to stimulate a pride in the state and motivate reluctant readers interested in sports to read.

Note that the name of each athlete listed is followed by his hometown (if he is a native of Illinois) or his team affiliation. Annotations include reference to appropriate pages or to the index of a book only if more than one athlete, sport, or team are dealt with; page or index references are omitted when an entire book deals with a particular athlete or team. Appropriate grade levels are in parentheses. The symbol "OP" identifies out-of-print books.

Team Sports

Baseball

PLAYERS

Bottomley, Jim (Sunny Jim)   Oglesby, Ill.
     Devaney, John. *The Greatest Cardinals of Them All.*
     Putnam, 1968. p.40–42 (6–10)

Hartnett, Leo (Gabby)   Chicago Cubs
     Hirshberg, Al. *Baseball's Greatest Catchers.* Putnam, 1966. p.70–78 (6–10)

Kling, Johnny   Chicago Cubs
        Hirshberg, Al. *Baseball's Greatest Catchers*. Putnam,
        1966. p.20–28 (6–10)
Schalk, Ray   Chicago White Sox
        Hirshberg, Al. *Baseball's Greatest Catchers*. Putnam,
        1966. p.37–44 (6–10)
Schoendienst, Al (Red)   Germantown, Ill.
        Devaney, John. *The Greatest Cardinals of Them All*.
        Putnam, 1968. p.162–72 (6–10)
        Hirshberg, Al. *The Man Who Fought Back: Red
        Schoendienst*. Messner, 1961. (6–12) OP
        Schoor, Gene. *The Red Schoendienst Story*. Putnam,
        1961. (6–12) OP
Turley, Robert (Bob)   Troy and East St. Louis, Ill.
        Schoor, Gene. *Bob Turley: Fireball Pitcher*. Putnam,
        1959. (7–10) OP

        CLUBS

Chicago Cubs
        Anderson, Dave and Milton Lancelot. *Upset: The Un-
        expected in the World of Sports*. Doubleday, 1967.
        p.109–11 (7–12)
        Hirshberg, Al. *Baseball's Greatest Catchers*. Putnam,
        1966. See index. (6–10)
Chicago White Sox
        Fitzgerald, Ed, ed. *The American League*. Grosset,
        1963. p.47–73 (8 up)
        Hirshberg, Al. *Baseball's Greatest Catchers*. Putnam,
        1966. See index. (6–10)

Basketball

        PLAYERS

Mikan, George   Joliet, Ill.
        Davis, Mac. *100 Greatest Sports Heroes*. Grosset,
        1954. p.80–81 (6–10)
        Hirshberg, Al. *Basketball's Greatest Stars*. Putnam,
        1963. p.9–19 (6–10)
        Hollander, Zander, comp. and ed. *Great American*

Athletes of the 20th Century. Random, 1966. p.97–99
(7–10)

Liss, Howard. *The Winners: National Basketball Association Championship Playoffs.* Delacorte, 1968. p.18–35, 43–63 (7–12)

Football

PLAYERS

Eckersall, Walter   Chicago, Ill.

Leckie, Robert. *The Story of Football.* Random, 1965. See index. (5–9)

Graham, Otto   Waukegan, Ill.

Devaney, John. *The Pro Quarterbacks.* Putnam, 1966. See index. (6–10)

Heuman, William. *Famous Pro Football Stars.* Dodd, 1967. p.111–19 (7–10)

Hollander, Zander, comp. and ed. *Great American Athletes of the 20th Century.* Random, 1966. p.52–54 (7–10)

Grange, Harold (Red)   Wheaton, Ill.

Davis, Mac. *100 Greatest Sports Heroes.* Grosset, 1954. p.46–47 (6–10)

Heuman, William. *Famous American Athletes.* Dodd, 1963. p.81–91 (6–10)

Heuman, William. *Famous Pro Football Stars.* Dodd, 1967. p.44–57 (7–10)

Hollander, Zander, comp. and ed. *Great American Athletes of the 20th Century.* Random, 1966. p.55–58 (7–10)

Leckie, Robert. *The Story of Football.* Random, 1965. See index. (5–9)

Schoor, Gene. *Red Grange: Football's Greatest Halfback.* Messner, 1952. (7–10) OP

Luckman, Sid   Chicago, Ill.

Devaney, John. *The Pro Quarterbacks.* Putnam, 1966. p.37–54 (7–10)

COACHES

Stagg, Amos Alonzo   University of Chicago

125

Davis, Mac. *100 Greatest Sports Heroes.* Grosset, 1954.
p.120–21 (6–10)

Leckie, Robert. *The Story of Football.* Random, 1965.
See index. (5–9)

Zuppke, Robert (Bob)   University of Illinois

Leckie, Robert. *The Story of Football.* Random, 1965.
See index. (5–9)

TEAMS

Chicago Bears

Anderson, Dave and Milton Lancelot. *Upset: The
Unexpected in the World of Sports.* Doubleday, 1967.
p.13–17 (7–12)

Devaney, John. *The Pro Quarterbacks.* Putnam, 1966.
See index. (6–10)

Heuman, William. *Famous Pro Football Stars.* Dodd,
1967. p.52–56, 97–101 (7–10)

Hollander, Zander, comp. and ed. *Great American
Athletes of the 20th Century.* Random, 1966. p.77–79
(7–10)

Izenberg, Jerry. *Championship: The Complete NFL
Title Story.* Four Winds, 1966. p.1–11, 19–22, 30–43,
51–54, 88–91, 118–23 (7–10) OP

Leckie, Robert. *The Story of Football.* Random, 1965.
See index. (5–9)

Chicago Cardinals

Izenberg, Jerry. *Championship: The Complete NFL
Title Story.* Four Winds, 1966. p.55–61 (7–10) OP

University of Chicago

Leckie, Robert. *The Story of Football.* Random, 1965.
See index. (5–9)

University of Illinois

Leckie, Robert. *The Story of Football.* Random, 1965.
See index. (5–9)

Hockey

PLAYERS

Hull, Bobby   Chicago Black Hawks

O'Brien, Andy. *Young Hockey Champions.* Norton, 1969. p.16–26 (5–9)

Sullivan, George. *Hockey Heroes: The Game's Great Players.* Garrard, 1969. p.9–41 (4–6)

Mikita, Stan   Chicago Black Hawks

O'Brien, Andy. *Young Hockey Champions.* Norton, 1969. p.1–15 (5–9)

TEAMS

Chicago Black Hawks

Anderson, Dave and Milton Lancelot. *Upset: The Unexpected in the World of Sports.* Doubleday, 1967. p.130–33 (7–12)

Individual Sports

Billiards

Greenleaf, Ralph   Monmouth, Ill.

Davis, Mac. *100 Greatest Sports Heroes.* Grosset, 1954. p.48 (6–10)

Bowling

Garms, Shirley Rudolph   Chicago Area

Jacobs, Helen. *Famous American Women Athletes.* Dodd, 1964. p.38–44 (7–9)

Boxing

Ross, Barney   Chicago, Ill.

Pizer, Vernon. *Glorious Triumphs: Athletes Who Conquered Adversity.* Dodd, 1966, 1968. p.1–22 (6–10)

Broad jump

Owens, James (Jesse)   Chicago, Ill.

Heuman, William. *Famous American Athletes.* Dodd, 1963. p.99–106 (6–10)

Hollander, Zander, comp. and ed. *Great American Athletes of the 20th Century.* Random, 1966. p.115–17 (7–10)

Pole vault

Richards, Robert (Bob)   Champaign, Ill.
    Heuman, William. *Famous American Athletes*. Dodd,
    1963. p.123–28 (6–10)

Swimming

Weissmuller, John (Johnny)   Chicago, Ill.
    Davis, Mac. *100 Greatest Sports Heroes*. Grosset,
    1954. p.137 (6–10)
    Gelman, Steve. *Young Olympian Champions*. Norton,
    1964. p.13–25 (5–10)
    Heuman, William. *Famous American Athletes*. Dodd,
    1963. p.93–98 (6–10)
    Hollander, Zander, comp. and ed. *Great American
    Athletes of the 20th Century*. Random, 1966. p.152–
    55 (7–10)